BRITANNIA TO
BEIRA AND
BEYOND

By

Mike Critchley

First published 2010
ISBN 978-1-904459-42-2

© Maritime Books 2010
Published by Maritime Books, Lodge Hill, Liskeard, PL14 4EL
Printed in England

Visit the Maritime Books website at www.navybooks.com

ACKNOWLEDGEMENTS

Without some gentle nudging from one of my three daughters some years ago this book would never have been written. Thanks girls.....but it was meant to be for my grandchildren - who have yet to appear!!

I must also express my thanks to Rear Admiral David Eckersley-Maslin who provided much information and photographs regarding my time under his command in HMS EASTBOURNE. His memory and diaries were far better than mine! He was, incidentally, somewhat alarmed to read of the "Queen Mary incident" (see page 145) revealed to him for the very first time when the book was at its proof stage. I certainly didn't have the courage to do it at the time.

My thanks to to the staff of the National Archives and Naval Historical Branch who produced documents from my past (and unseen by me for forty years) that enabled facts to be checked and my memory jogged.

A huge thank you must go to Sue Weller who read my original work and highlighted the many paragraphs where only a naval reader would understand what I had written. She has done a great job to edit it so it can, I trust, be understood by those who have no naval knowledge or background.

To my staff at Maritime Books – Pat Garnett and Steve Bush – who have brought the book to a format ready for a printer – a big thank you too.

...and thank you for buying a copy!

Contents

INTRODUCTION

As a publisher of naval books for nearly 25 years I have frequently advised potential authors who seek advice about writing their memoirs. I always suggest they write such a document but advise them not to invest in paying to have copies printed: 'Just a few photocopies for the family for when you cross the bar,' has always been my recommendation.

But do I follow my own advice? Well... here I am having returned home from Malta where I locked myself in a hotel room and furiously typed away at what will, I trust, be seen as some sort of humourous memoir of the first five years of a fantastic Royal Naval career. Perhaps more could follow?

There was a serious side to my time spent in uniform but I have tried to focus on the good times, as one should. Endless patrols and exercises don't make interesting reading, whether they could be best described as indifferent, 100% boring, simply horrid or frankly frightening. I trust what follows raises the odd wry smile and perhaps encourages some other young people to engage in a naval career. It isn't all 'fun in the sun' and there is very much another more serious side to a career afloat but you can have a great laugh with some great people too – that's a promise!

So... these were my old Maltese haunts; streets and creeks so familiar (now full of yachts rather than warships), and a great place to return to from all the distractions of home life to put this book together. I hope you enjoy it.

Can I apologise for any errors of facts forty years after the events recounted here. I have done my best – but the mistakes are all mine too!

Mike Critchley
Sliema Malta 2010

CHAPTER ONE

YOU CAN BLAME IT ON CURLY - OR WAS IT DONALD?

You can blame Curly – or was it Donald?

I was just one of so many young boys for whom there was no other proper career in life but to be a sailor… in some capacity or other. Living by the sea on the very edge of a busy Naval port I observed the Royal Navy on almost a daily basis so I guess the recruiters didn't have to work too hard to grab my attention in later life. But it was up to Curly or Donald to decide the initial way forward for me…

I was eight years old and living in Gosport when my parents decided I should cross the harbour to Portsmouth by ferry every day to be educated at Portsmouth Grammar School. As a mere slip of a child I decided, even before my first visit, that Portsmouth Grammar was not to my liking. For a start I had to get up far too early, take a bus to the ferry terminal, cross the harbour by ferry in all weathers and then tackle the long walk to the school at Cambridge Junction. This was definitely not my idea of fun, but parental wishes had to be obeyed!

The highlight of my day was often the ferry crossing, especially on really foggy days when the skipper (without the advantage of radar, of course) refused to take the VADNE or FERRY QUEEN across the short but busy stretch of water. We (a great mob of us aged from eight to eighteen years old) were thus sent home for the day. Far better than a Physics or Latin lesson!

What really excited us kids however was when Curly was on duty. As one of several crew members of the ferry he actually took time to talk to us schoolboys, chatting about his work and our day. When we arrived at our destination he even attempted to preserve us from the crush of dockyard workers and their bicycles, which made up the major part of the passengers on most days, by telling them in no uncertain terms to 'hold back while the youngsters get off.' As time progressed, and with suitable training, Curly would allow us to pick up the huge manila rope that secured the vessel after each short journey, and heave it at the pontoon bollard as the vessel approached. He trained a number of us up quite well, doubtless in defiance of all the rules! If we secured the rope on the first attempt all was well but, as passengers were not prepared to be delayed by even a few seconds, near misses were never appreciated. My seamanship training had started....

Although it may have been Curly who gave me the first taste of a future seagoing career, my maternal grandfather was also to blame. Home at that time was a house that grandfather had built and into which my parents had moved when they married. Grandmother had died some years previously and so my grandfather was on his own. My father was away in the RAF so this arrangement was considered ideal for my mother and me. Our home backed onto one of the inlets, or creeks, of Portsmouth Harbour, and at almost every opportunity grandfather would recount salty stories of his seagoing career as a Carpenter and later Shipwright Officer in the Royal Navy. At his knee I learnt all about the sea, which also happened to be, literally, at the bottom of the family garden.

Grandfather taught me to sail when I was eight or nine in a large clinker-built dinghy he built himself. Myself and the rest of the wider family, who came to stay every summer, held the good ship Donald in highest regard. We explored most of the inlets of Portsmouth harbour onboard in those balmy days of the 1950's.

The sea ran in our family, but with a tragic twist; I was never to meet my paternal grandfather who was also a Shipwright Officer. He drowned when HMS GOOD HOPE was sunk in the South Atlantic on 1st November 1914, along with nine hundred other souls on that terrible day. His widow gave birth to twin sons just five months later; one of them, Leonard, was to become my father. Perhaps that's why father chose a career in the RAF; the sea and the German Navy had indeed been cruel to him and his family. His mother had married, been widowed and given birth to twins, in that order, all within twelve cruel months.

Father himself survived a ditching in the Solent in his flying days in the air force when his plane fell from the sky and somersaulted into the water. It was a memorable day for me as a child to visit the local Portsmouth newspaper office with my father as he delved into the records to find the reports of his rescue.

What could best be described as an 'average' school career progressed and I gained promotion from rope thrower on the Gosport ferry to Leading Seaman in the school's Combined Cadet Force (Naval Section) – a promotion of far greater importance to me than any clutch of GCE exam results that were to follow. Days at sea in Motor Fishing Vessels on the Clyde, and Sea Days spent in ships such as H M ships BROADSWORD and CAUNTON were fine, but a week at sea in DUNDAS and later the WIZARD decided it for me. I wanted a career in the Royal Navy, and it didn't particularly matter what as - either as a sailor or officer would do.

It simply didn't matter to a sixteen-year-old; I would have been perfectly happy to sign up as an Able Seaman. However, my parents had other ideas; they saw me as a potential Officer and so I remained at school for the absolute minimum amount of time necessary to get the required brace of GCE certificates. How I struggled with those lectures... there were ships to sail on, oceans to cross, so why on earth did I need to go to Physics, Music or countless other lessons? Oxbridge was definitely not on the horizon!

In due course our careers master, a retired Colonel Willis, encouraged me to apply for a place at Dartmouth Royal Naval College, as did so many other Portsmouth Grammar pupils at that same time. I found I was both qualified and medically fit but, alas, too young by a mere few months! I knew it wouldn't be a rest cure but still, I was determined to at least apply. The entry age at that time was seventeen and a half years and I simply wasn't old enough. As I had no intention of staying on at school a minute longer it was to be the big wide world of work for me, whilst hoping for an interview that would lead to my being trained as a Royal Naval officer. If the Duke of Edinburgh and a whole host of Admirals could do it – so could I.

In those days there was no lack of jobs for a teenager and being a Christmas postman I found out was always great fun and a 'nice little earner'. Incidentally, I would like to apologise here for the hedges in my home town of Alverstoke I demolished on my Post Office bike while making short cuts between smart houses, or for those Christmas cards that all went back in the nearest red post box at 3pm when it was time to retire to the local Mocambo coffee bar, when the local girls were on the scene.

My prayers (and I certainly believed in them) were answered and in due course an envelope arrived inviting me to attend the Admiralty Interview Board at HMS SULTAN, conveniently situated just a few hundred yards from the family home in Privett Road. Some thirty of us arrived for three or four days of interviews and aptitude tests, all presided over by no less than a real Admiral. It was to be no push over.

The tests were stringent and as each day passed our numbers decreased; those considered unacceptable were discreetly offered a lift to the railway station to begin the long haul home and, it was widely rumoured, an application form for the Army or RAF to take with them. At least the queue for breakfast grew shorter each morning.

Seemingly endless interviews and aptitude tests, with a diverse range of people from headmasters to psychiatrists to senior naval officers, went on for days and culminated in an initiative test in an old aircraft hangar. A simulated 'river' was painted on the floor of the hangar flowing from one wall to the other. A massive supply of oil drums, planks, ropes and spars were provided for us to bridge the river in whatever fashion we thought best. When we found that the planks were all a fraction too short for the required job we realised why this morning's fun and games was known as the initiative test.

By now there were about ten of us left. We had to devise and then instigate a master plan to get our group across the river using only the props provided. Before the fun started we were encouraged to warm up by kicking a couple of footballs around the hanger. A whistle indicated warm up time was over and for the balls to be returned to the supervising Physical Training Instructor (PTI). As the nearest person to one of the balls I gave it an almighty boot that should have earned me a place in the Premier League. Mind you, I was no sportsman and here was my chance to prove it… the fluke ball hurtled half the length of the hangar, past the PTI and straight towards a door that, with perfect yet unfortunate timing, opened to reveal the Admiral in full uniform. The ball slammed into his neck, just a few inches from hitting him full in the face. I assumed I would be asked to leave the place and find my way home in the footsteps of all the other interviewees who were never going to be naval officers…

It seemed that the shadow of a smile passed over his face but I knew I was a marked man from this point for the rest of my time at SULTAN. I dreaded meeting the Admiral again, yet if I was considered half suitable I knew it was inevitable that our paths would cross.

My nerves meant that for me lunch was a light affair as I prepared to meet the big man and a host of his supporting cast for my final interview. I knocked at his door and was ordered into an unnervingly big office. The required pleasantries were exchanged and if the Admiral's neck was red as a result of my indiscretion then my face certainly matched it. His first question was, 'I see you left school a while ago. What have you been doing since?'

Perhaps this was the moment to expound my full and chequered career to date. It was fairly unremarkable: paint sprayer at a Gosport factory (five weeks) BP petrol pump attendant at Rowner (six weeks) strawberry picking at Titchfield (three weeks) plus the great Christmas postal job. That certainly wouldn't have him signing my score sheet for automatic entry to Dartmouth. No, I had to come up with the honest answer for my current employment.

'Well sir,' I sputtered. 'Do you know Privett Road, sir? Just a few hundred yards away, sir?'

He did.

'Well sir, I live there, and I painted the white line down the centre of it last week.' I offered my upturned hands towards the board just to let them see the evidence: despite a week of a teenager's fervent washing I still had some of the evidence around my fingernails to prove my statement. I guess they believed me; as far as I know they never did take up references from that particular pre-naval employment opportunity.

To this day I know not why, but only four of us out of around thirty hopefuls passed our four-day interrogation. A few days later a letter arrived offering me a place at Her Majesty's Britannia Royal Naval College Dartmouth. My mother didn't really want to let her only child go at what was, to her, the tender age of seventeen but neither she, nor my father, stood in my way.

Curly would have been so proud of me. To think that all that rope throwing had lead me to the gates of Dartmouth College.

CHAPTER TWO

SO, DARTMOUTH HERE I COME

Like generations of young men before me I reported to Platform Three at Paddington Railway Station in London on the appointed day, 6th January 1963. Time to board the train heading west to Kingswear for Dartmouth and yet another career, a proper one this time. Would this one last longer than my best record to date… a mere six weeks?

I was by now just five days older than the lower age limit for entry into the Navy – no one could surely be younger. So started a big adventure for a very young, doubtless very spotty-faced, Gosport lad.

There was time to spare before the train left so I tore myself away from the other budding future First Sea Lords assembled on the station platform to sneak to the head of the train to take a look at the fine King class loco building up a good head of steam in preparation for its dash to the west. The thought crossed my mind that I could always apply to learn to drive one of these if warships turned out not to be my forte.

Despite these second thoughts I eventually boarded the train and arrived at Kingswear railway station four hours later with a motley crew of new recruits, seemingly from all corners of the world. That January evening's crossing of the river to Dartmouth by ferry boat was simply memorable as the college sat majestically above the town, partially illuminated and partially lost in a low cloud of a winter evening's sea mist rolling up the river.....

Within minutes of landing we loaded our suitcases on to a naval lorry for the ride up to the college, except, first surprise - we humans didn't get the ride; transport was for the suitcases only! We were 'fallen in' and a poor Gunnery Instructor had the thankless and almost impossible task of marching in formation a straggling group of raw teenagers up the long winding hill to the college, few of who had ever marched anywhere in their lives, let alone in step.

As a recently retired Leading Seaman (Combined Cadet Force) I was overcome with embarrassment as we stumbled past a few Dartmouth locals out taking the evening air. We eventually made it up the hill to the college and the huge wooden doors that led from the Parade ground into the college building slammed firmly shut behind us. We had arrived... we were indeed very close to being 'in the navy now'.

As those of that generation remember, the winter of 1963 was something else throughout much of the country. Snow blanketed South Devon for many weeks, and not just a passing dusting; we are talking tons and tons of the white stuff. For those of us from the UK it can best be described as 'somewhat different': the majority of my class, I soon discovered, were from Nigeria, Ghana and Malaysia, so for them snow and a major drop in temperature from what they had experienced in their home countries just days earlier before they flew to the UK to start their training was, for many, beyond a joke. However, they were not excused from mustering on the parade ground shortly after 0600 to be given shovels suitably adapted to move the stuff. 'Just get out there and shift it,' came the order. Many of them were from privileged backgrounds in their home countries and I doubt if they had ever lifted much more than a glass of chilled water, let alone a shovel.

'Early Morning Activities' started shortly after 0600 and included such delights as boat work on the river, swimming rigorous lengths of the pool, or early morning parade training on the very impressive parade ground in front of the college. When the said parade ground is beneath two feet of snow you can only guess what went through the minds of the Nigerian cadets when invited to start shovelling the stuff off the tarmac as the sun rose. Just days before they had been enjoying the heat in their homeland. Many of my African classmates couldn't cope with the inadequate central heating system in the dormitories so they moved into, and took over, the drying rooms of the college where normally the rugby shirts were hung out to dry.

The college has been going since 1905 and we slotted into the normal college activities that had been well tested and tried by many generations of cadets before us. Physical fitness, endless naval and academic lectures, plus private studies, resulted in a packed schedule and by 2000 each evening most of us were desperate to crawl into our dormitory bunk beds, but before we could do that other chores awaited us. We always seemed to end our waking hours polishing boots, clearing up our accommodation areas and completing work books that we just hadn't had time to finish during the day. There was never a moment free to sit about and think, be it about home, a career elsewhere or even time at sea, should we ever be fortunate enough to complete our training.

The overall theory at Dartmouth was that we had to be trained to do anything that one day we might ask sailors we would command to do. One highlight that sticks in the memory was the delight of the evening initiative test. It always started without any warning when a class or group was instructed to meet at the main gate of the college. Some already in bed rapidly grabbed the appointed uniform 'rig of the day' and headed for the appointed rendezvous. A lorry ticking over in the cark park, its exhaust wafting away on the frosty night air always meant we were off on an initiative test.

Our first test started at a drop-off point in the tiny hamlet of East Portlemouth opposite the holiday resort of Salcombe. Late on a February night it could hardly be described as welcoming, but the few lights glowing in the handful of houses that we passed made the snow look attractive, even if you had just jumped from the back of a lorry that only had a basic thin canvas cover to protect its human cargo. One wag onboard, who obviously had a relative who had served under these conditions for weeks on Russian Convoy duties in World War II, reminded us of the fact. It almost made the snow feel warm, but not quite.

Our briefing came from an instructor, well prepared with woolly hat, thermos, heavy-duty greatcoat and the ever-present clipboard. We had found ourselves on a beach 'behind enemy lines,' he said, and had a few 'simple exercises' to carry out during the night; meet a few 'friendly agents', carry out their instructions and all would be well. Even before we started our group reported mirages of our iron framed beds at the college calling out for them to return...

Our first test was to go to the beach at East Portlemouth where each group of four cadets was 'invited' to take six pounds of sand to Start Point some ten miles away! Yes, we had maps, but first of all we had to find the beach and sand some-where under all that snow. Of course we had nothing in which to carry the sand, and no idea of what six pounds of sand looked like. The dustmen must have been to East Portlemouth earlier that day; creeping into the slumbering residents' gardens we attempted, quietly, to liberate the contents of their dustbins in the hope of a suitable container, but they were all empty.

The clock was running… where else could we find a container, sand for the carrying of, at such an hour of the night? There was no other way forward – it was off with my trousers. Why mine? Well, the Malaysians said they couldn't 'for religious reasons' (clever guys), and all the others were older and/or bigger than me so there wasn't much choice. A quick knot in each trouser leg and, having cleared the snow away with our bare and rapidly freezing hands, we filled each trouser leg with the best (but very wet and heavy) sand that dozens of holiday-makers had enjoyed the previous summer. This sand was for 'clandestine military purposes', not for your bucket and spade brigade.

We were ready. Our Nigerian guide, who had been selected by our seniors to be our leader that night, headed off into the pitch darkness with just the glimmer of moonlight on the snow to pick out the minor roads and pathways that would, we planned, eventually lead us to the lighthouse at Start Point, flashing oh so faintly away in the distance. If this was an initiative test we were at a loss as to what initiative we could bring to bear as we trudged down a very lonely 'B' road in South Devon very late that freezing February night. The moon's glow highlighting the goose pimples on my somewhat scrawny teenager's legs is a memory I am still trying to erase from my mind.

Thinking back to World War II heroes that we had read about we pondered if we would be able to jump a train and ride the buffer beam… or turn up at the local airport disguised as airport workers and stow away on a flight to freedom… or steal a motorbike (or twelve) and make a dash for the border… All these ideas kept our minds active but despite trying to muster all the 'initiative' we had in our chilled bodies none seemed relevant to our situation in South Devon that night. There was no choice but to keep trudging on towards the distant beckoning light-house. My major preoccupation was to keep my Y fronts hidden from any passing female teenagers who we may encounter that night; it wasn't, I am pleased to report, too difficult a task because on this pitch black February night the whole place was absolutely dead. Anyone with any sense was either in, or heading for, bed.

I never, ever want to see Start Point lighthouse again. We set off at a cracking pace to get to our first rendezvous, vaguely aware of the other teams in the gloom around us. (Why did someone pick a Nigerian to lead us on this pitch dark night, or was it some kind of joke?) At least no one understood what could only be presumed to be wild African oaths thrown out from our international team members' mouth as we ran, then marched, and then almost stumbled to the lighthouse. I know how uncomfortable I felt that night, so what thoughts crossed the minds of an African chief's son so far from home I can't even begin to guess. As we approached the vast eerie granite structure we spotted the car of the 'agent' we had to meet (it looked suspiciously similar to a vehicle we often saw in the officers' car park back at Dartmouth). The car was empty, but with its steamed up windows, a thermos of hot chocolate on the front passenger seat and the lilting strains of a concert playing on the car radio… it seemed we were back in the real world again.

Out leapt our 'agent'. We assumed he would point us to the lorry we had left earlier and that our beds were not too far away. None of it… the hot chocolate was his but no such luxuries for us; all we were given was a pair of domestic kitchen scales and we set about weighing our samples of East Portlemouth sand. We just stood back in amazement, fearful that if we didn't have enough we would be sent back to get more. My trousers had been well stuffed and aching shoulder muscles bore testimony to the fact as we had taken it in turns to get the sand to Start Point in our trouser 'neck-bags'.

The great sand weigh-in was conducted by torch light, and I then realised that six pounds of sand is not very much at all. Had we all filled our pockets rather than my trousers we could have fulfilled our instructor's requirements. Whatever… some 28 pounds of genuine East Portlemouth sand now lies somewhere at the foot of Start Point lighthouse!! But who cares… now, where was that lorry?

There was no lorry; it was pointed out that our next 'agent' was at Dartmouth Castle, a massive twelve or more miles away. Our hearts sank fast – what stroke of genius could we bring to bear now? Would we hitch a ride with a friendly farmer passing with a tractor and cart, at well past midnight? Why was there no bicycle rack we could liberate at Start Point? Why was the after-midnight bus service so poor? It was no good; we had no choice but to start walking again, just as soon as I had scrambled back into my cold, very damp and sandy trousers.

Hours later we stumbled into the very eerie remains of the castle that stands guard at the entrance to the River Dart. We had obviously taken far too long to complete the route march from Start Point, or maybe the agent had retreated to refill his thermos; anyway, we never did meet him that night. We thought we had used our initiative well and returned to the college to be greeted by our training officer who had waited up most of the night to meet this snow-covered group of scruffs. On falling us in back in at the college there wasn't a single word of congratulations on completing the course; we received a tirade of what would doubtless today be called verbal abuse. Our lack of moral fibre and initiative, failure to carry out the full instructions, were hammered home. As a parting shot before we collapsed into our beds in a state very close to exhaustion we were informed that as we had 'failed miserably' we would be required to go through a similar exercise again a few nights later. We were not even awarded an extra twenty minutes in bed. Dartmouth routines don't change; in just a few hours the sun rose feebly, as did we, and we were back on the river rowing a wretched whaler up and down as part of our normal physical education. I'm sure we needed it that morning after so many hours vegetating overnight in our bunks…

As promised, just a few days later the re-run of the initiative test was thrust upon us, with no warning of course. No sand this time, just a simple late night jog around the lanes of South Devon for a few miles, down to the River Dart a mile or so north of the college where our 'agent' told us four or five heavy 27ft whalers would be waiting for us to use. We had to cross the river to meet our next agent in a railway tunnel on the Paignton to Kingswear line. It was true, there were whalers on the riverbank for us to use, but they had been put there some hours earlier, and in the interval the tide had fallen by almost its full range. Time to take our trousers off, again. All of us this time!

We had to manhandle the whalers down to the river's edge for what was to be a very short crossing of the Dart. Our instructors had of course selected a patch of riverbank where the mud was at its blackest and thinnest. Good for the soul, they said, as the freezing mud reached up to our thighs. (Women I'm told pay money for all this mud stuff; did they learn something we missed that night?)

We eventually staggered up slippery riverbanks, met our man in the tunnel and even got a smile from the training officer. We surmised we had passed this hurdle. The full task was eventually completed and we made our way back to our bunks very early in the morning and were asleep in seconds.

Unbeknown to us at the time we were obviously going through the part of our training when, if we were going to leave the navy, it would have been administratively useful if we had thrown in the towel at this stage. I'm sure for some people it must have been a close call but no one did actually leave. We had got this far and a few very late nights, snow, wet sand and a pile of mud were not enough to distract us. Someone even called it all fun, but that word never did cross my lips – promise!

The other highlight still in my mind over forty years later was the joy of the boxing ring! I thought I was being trained at Dartmouth to perhaps fight at sea for my Queen and country but on one occasion it was decided we should all fight in the boxing ring too.

All the class were weighed on a pair of bathroom scales at the ringside, paired off with someone of the same weight and given boxing gloves to match. Someone found a ringside bell and a watch and we were in business. All the Brits were happy to rapidly form gentlemen's agreements whereby a few punches from Cadet Smith were returned by a few punches by Cadet Jones and both then just had to wait for the three minutes to tick by. No gentlemen's agreement for me and my Nigerian partner; the above 'rules' were quietly explained to him but the status of his entire nation was on the line here as far as he was concerned and he entered the ring at full power, as if he was the defending middleweight champion of Lagos (perhaps he was!!). Duckin' and divin' with well placed punches everywhere, it was the longest three minutes of my life and to this day I compliment myself on staying in a semi-conscious state to the bitter end!

At last the bell rang and I staggered from the ring with a little help from my seconds. Flopping on a ringside bench my mates came over to compliment me on my newfound skills but from the corner of my eye I could see my training officer approach. He too was surely going to compliment me for my best shot against the middleweight champ of Lagos? Not so... he simply bent over this recovering cadet and whispered that my hair was far too long and I was to report to his office the next day having visited the barber's in the interval. Not a word of congratulation again. Over the years I have kept up my visits to the barber, but have never been back in the boxing ring.

At this point in the long history of the Royal Navy much senior officers' planning effort was being focused on the Polaris missile submarine project. After the Cuban missile crisis of 1962 there was an urgent requirement to build four nuclear-powered submarines to enable the Royal Navy to take the Polaris nuclear intercontinental deterrent to sea. A huge complicated submarine building programme was underway, and the word at Dartmouth was obviously to get cadets 'thinking submarines' as the programme was going to need a much larger intake of potential submariners than had been the norm in previous years.

So within a very few weeks of getting a uniform on our backs we were sitting on an ancient navy bus heading for the submarine escape training tank at Gosport. In later years a trip to a submarine in the Bahamas may be thought of as a good 'carrot' to dangle in front of impressionable teenagers. We had no such carrot; we were all plonked on a bus and off we went to the dreaded 'tank'. As generations of submariners know, the tank is a huge 100ft structure dominating the Gosport skyline where escape drills are conducted. The thinking is that, should a submarine lie crippled on the seabed, there is the possibility that by using various methods men can indeed escape from their stricken vessel.

A mock-up portion of a submarine at ground level has a tank full of water rising no less than 100ft above the escape compartment. When the escapees, equipped only with swimming trunks and a life jacket, are ready in the escape compartment water is allowed to flood it. Eventually the air pressure in the chamber is compressed by the water flooding in. The rush of water soon stops and, breathing this compressed air, the escapers are ready to ascend. For this seventeen-year-old the whole process looked positively horrific. Fortunately for me at the point before entering the torture chamber the escape tank doctor took a look in all our ears and decreed that I couldn't make the ascent. A common cold was all that was needed to render the ascent unwise. As he reported the fact to the tank staff I could have leapt forward and kissed the Doc. Never in my life since has a doctor given me better news than the common cold diagnosis that day. I had no wish to volunteer to repeat the exercise and vowed to have a cold for the rest of my time at Dartmouth.

Classed as 'medically unfit' I was allowed to go to the top of the tank to watch my classmates make their death-defying acts of heroism. Perhaps the pre-escape briefing was not the best. Our African classmates could not have been listening to the very clear instructions given; they were told to simply breathe out when clear of the escape chamber. (Why they had to carry out this training is another issue, as their Navy simply didn't have any submarines.)

The compressed air in the escapee's lungs has to be spewed out as he ascends to prevent a burst lung on the way up and, despite the knowledge of the vast amount of water above, the air available just keeps on coming as air expands and speed is gained on the rapid upwards ascent... There is of course a natural reluctance to breathe out too much air too soon, a problem solved by instructors lurking in the tank to give escapees a fine belt in the stomach as they passed.

It was an amazing sight seeing one's fellow classmates hurtle out of the water as they reached the top of this tower. To this day I am thankful that a simple cold prevented my 'escape' but salute those who not only carry out escape training but also earn their pay under the waves as a career. Not for me guys!

I returned to Dartmouth a 'failure' – phew! It felt so good... But the Navy still wanted its quota of new submariners. They hadn't given up hope with any of us yet...

Shortly after the submarine experience we were next to 'enjoy' the Minesweeper experience. Packed off to Portland we were soon to grab our first forty-eight hours of 'sea experience' a la Grey funnel line. It's not quite the same as P&O offer their customers. Fortunately, it wasn't too long before we were back at Dartmouth as our tiny Minesweeper, HMS WOTTON, introduced us to little more than experience in the English Channel in the winter. Perhaps it would have been better had I taken the other advice my careers masters gave... We all did a lot of talking to Hughie as we crossed Lyme Bay depositing breakfasts overboard as we went.

One lighter interlude in the training schedule came on a Sunday evening when, with no instructions or boot cleaning to occupy our time, and with preparations for the following Monday morning completed it was time to relax.

For my class, dancing was the only option available! A dear lady from Kingswear arrived each Sunday evening on the hallowed quarterdeck with a small portable wind-up gramophone player, a clutch of records and boundless enthusiasm to teach the up-and-coming generation of young naval officers the intricacies of... yes, ballroom dancing! Ugh. I had never danced a single step in my life and in all honesty wasn't over keen to learn. The desire to learn was also greatly overshadowed by the fact that 95% of the rest of the college had no scheduled activities on a Sunday evening so the hot word went round that the balcony above the quarterdeck was an ideal vantage point to watch twenty of their compatriots make complete fools of themselves.

The whole of the procedure would doubtless have been greatly enhanced had any young ladies been on hand to provide partners but that wasn't to be. The naval training regime didn't stretch that far. For us it was quite a problem – but not for our intrepid dancing guru. We were instantly paired off with each other, one cadet nominated to be the female partner. There was no way my huge Nigerian opposite number was going to act in the female role. Towering a good six inches above me his statement 'Me man... you woman,' was quite straightforward and to the point. I knew the steps I was meant to take as the portable record player did its best in the cavernous environment of the college and I stumbled about the place led by my strapping African.

As the comments started to hurtle down from the viewing gallery above, it was more than difficult to take this part of our training with anything other than a huge pinch of salt, which is doubtless why to this day I have no dancing skills whatsoever. But ladies, should you ever be looking for a traditional ballroom dancing partner, especially if you happen to be passing through northern Nigeria, I can suggest a few names who may be suitable and perhaps even available...

Don't you just love them... someone had to do the job, but the Parade Training staff were never the most popular members of the instructional team. In the college classrooms if (or more accurately when) we made a mistake we had a friendly staff member soon alongside us explaining what we had done wrong and how it could be done better next time. On the Parade ground however it was totally different. Place your left boot three inches out of line with the other fourteen left boots in the squad and it seemed as if World War III had been declared. A rampant Gunnery Instructor (GI) would bellow all sorts of profanities doubting one's parentage... promising all manner of punishment... hinting that the end of one's new career was at hand – and all because one's big left hand boot was slightly misaligned. Hey ho, it's a funny old world...

One Lieutenant Bill Smith RN, who we noted had a Distinguished Service Medal (DSM) after his name, led the parade ground team. We later researched a little and discovered it was an award for service as a human torpedo crew member during World War II. He was a warm friendly Yorkshire man, pure gold. We were both later to serve in the same ship together as fellow officers but, for now, the relationship was very much instructor and instructed.

If Bill Smith was one of life's gentlemen it is more than could be said for some of his staff. One particular Petty Officer had no love of this, his last draft in the Navy. He made it very clear he had no wish to be on the Dartmouth parade ground at 0630 in the snow (did he seriously think we wanted to be there?)...had no wish to be in the Navy... and certainly no wish to be trying to instil the art of parade training into a bunch of potential officers gently freezing in front of him. We all made a mental note that we had no wish to remain in the company of this little unhappy soul either. The Royal Navy it seemed wasn't big enough for all of us!

Like all good things even parade training and the rest of our time at the college came to an end. It was time to head off to sea and our 'initial sea training'...

CHAPTER THREE

TENBY TIME

The ageing Type 12 frigate HMS TENBY lay idly at her berth in Devonport Dockyard. The once frontline frigate had been refitted as a young officers' training ship and thus downgraded to 'secondary duties' within the Fleet. A fair proportion of her normal ship's company had been sent off to other ships, their places taken by an after mess deck full of cadets and a group of Royal Marine Young Officers from the Commando Training establishment at Lympstone in South Devon. As the Navy's future 'Sea Soldiers' they too were at the early stage of their training when three months' sea experience was considered appropriate for them. In fact, we treated them as a bunch of passengers: they just didn't want to be there – they would have been far happier in a trench on Dartmoor pretending to be soldiers. They were world experts at going to sleep – anywhere - and often we ended up doing the work intended for them, which didn't help relationships between us.

We had our summer leave to look forward to after Dartmouth before the beginning of the next phase in September. Before leaving the college we exchanged stories with the more senior members (by about three months!) of the college about their 'Training Squadron time'. Some had been on a three month navigational training cruise to the West Indies; others enjoyed the delights of Scandinavia in mid-summer, while others 'just' spent their three months cruising the Med each weekday and recovering at the weekend in ports we had only seen in holiday brochures. So, encouraged by these stories, we were all looking forward to our time away from the college; some real sea time and overseas adventures too! We also looked even further ahead to when we could return home and impress our old school friends (those with more mundane jobs) with our salty stories from the ocean deep and, hopefully, our suntans as evidence!

But as we left Dartmouth that summer for our August leave, stories started to circulate that our cruise was to be 'Home and European waters.' Maybe our dreams were not to be realised! Surely some mistake had been made?

On arrival back at Devonport in September and after joining HMS TENBY we were able to confirm the stories were indeed true. No one issued us with tropical clothing or offered to jab us for diseases we had never heard of; we were simply greeted with a notice board displaying the somewhat bland outline of our planned programme for the autumn. Portland in September, The Clyde in October, and Portsmouth in November interspersed with the delights of just two foreign visits – all the way to Ghent in Belgium and Brest in France. Wouldn't we have some stories to tell our friends when we got back home! Wouldn't we just…

The well-tried and tested theory of the Dartmouth Training Squadron was to take cadets to sea and get them to do every routine job that would normally be done by a junior rating. If we couldn't do the job today how could we expect one of our men to do a similar job when we were 'real' officers (hopefully) tomorrow? Even though we always seemed to end up with the dirtiest and most awkward of jobs it was, as the training staff frequently told us, 'good for the soul'.

Our Training Officer, one Lieutenant Mike Hare, was a congenial and fair man – we could ask for no more. As we got increasingly excited looking down the list of ports we could expect to visit – Greenock, Portland in Dorset, Brest, Ghent - news came through that a technical problem in the engineering department would prevent us from sailing and, whilst the regular ship's company were given an extra weekend leave, we would have an 'initiative test'. Not another! Once again I could feel myself trudging trouser-less through the snow of South Devon to deliver sand to a lighthouse… or maybe this time we would be dragging huge whalers through the midst of some new riverbed after dark…

Each of us was paired off with another trainee to await the staff who would bring our envelopes containing instructions for the weekend. My colleague David de Vere was a fresh-faced young man from Bath who was always game for a laugh….. Our excitement that blustery September day was similar to that experienced, I'm sure, by TV quiz show winners whilst the hostess takes a few seconds to present them with an envelope that would outline their prize. The anticipation was excruciating. Well, almost as exciting…

Out came our envelope… It included a railway warrant for two (one way) from Ebbw Vale to Plymouth; how exciting could this get? The second sheet of paper outlined our task: using our own initiative (of course) we were to find our own way to that unfamiliar Welsh town and carry out three tasks over the weekend.

We were to return by Monday morning having researched and written out the life history of the Welsh political leader Aneurin Bevan, collected a rubber stamp from the local police station to prove we had been on their patch, and interviewed the local postmistress.

As we threw a few clothes in a weekend holdall David and I mused how to use our God-given initiative to complete the task. Agreeing that 'if it's initiative they want it's initiative they'll get,' we jumped on a local bus outside the dockyard and headed for the city centre. As we sped into the reference department of the local library the very pretty young assistant was delighted to help two eager young teenagers in their research of a past political leader from the Welsh valleys. She scurried from tome to tome, unearthing more and more material; doubtless she hadn't seen a customer all day. Within twenty minutes we had more information before us than we would ever need, indeed enough to complete a university thesis on the good man. We lacked the courage to ask her to write it out over the weekend for us, but such was her enthusiasm I suspect she might have even done just that.

Our pens raced away as we found and copied word for word huge segments from the assembled books. Within little more than an hour we had completed our first task to our entire satisfaction and hadn't even left the Plymouth city boundary…

With a few pounds in our pockets to feed ourselves, we were soon standing close to the main A38 road from Plymouth, thumbs outstretched, trusty holdalls beside us with a borrowed sailor's hat firmly attached for all passing drivers to see. We'd been told that drivers would stop for a sailor's hat but never an officer's, and it certainly worked for us! As we headed east in the comfort of a kind person's car the thought of a weekend at David's parents home in Bath began to seem far more attractive than flogging up a Welsh mining valley. Once again we used our initiative as our plan took shape; yes, we would miss out Ebbw Vale, we decided, and head straight for Bath. We contrived, in true Colditz style, that we could forge a rubber stamp from the local police station and certainly it would be easy enough to concoct a piece of fiction as far as the interview with the postmistress was concerned…

27

Saturday morning in Bath was spent in David's home employing our very best forgery work for the rubber stamp from the Duty Sergeant at Ebbw Vale Police Station. After three attempts we produced what we considered to be a perfect job, complete with a small water splash so that it didn't look pristine. We proudly put it in a wallet, safely tucked away for presentation back onboard. We had no doubt whatsoever it was an excellent job!

We then set to work on the life history of the postmistress... One of three daughters from a mining family, wartime service in the land army, civil service exams, wedding to a soldier returned from the war, training course at the main Post Office in Swansea, many years spent at an idyllic post office on the Gower while raising her family, and the pre-retirement final move to the Post Office at Ebbw Vale, 'where we meet her this fine September morning...' It was a great piece of prose. Not only would we convince our training officer of a job well done, we anticipated any prizes that were on offer would be coming our way.

Having made the most of our initiative we spent the remainder of the weekend in Bath relaxing and watching TV - so much better than flogging down some windswept Welsh valley. Then, towards midnight on the Sunday, we headed off to the railway station, happy and confident to exchange our rail warrants enabling us to begin the journey back to Plymouth. The place was deserted and we soon realised we had missed the last train west. Much more than initiative was now required; we needed help from someone, and quickly! No point in producing our rail warrants; instead, armed with just our naval identity cards and a sob story about young officers and their initiative tests, we went to work on any official we could find.

All to no avail. We were within minutes of giving up and phoning the ship to admit our deceit and await further orders, anticipating arrest for desertion, when one of the station staff came up and told us that at some unearthly hour the night mail train to Plymouth would stop at Bath for a while, so 'It may be worth asking the supervisor to see if you could jump onboard and sleep on the sacks.' It seemed a reasonable plan, even though the whole of the country was reeling from news reports of what was to become known as the Great Train Robbery. It had taken place just a few days before we found ourselves on Bath railway station at well past midnight, idly waiting for a mail train. It could only happen to us!

We were dozing on the platform as the train rumbled in and stopped in front of us. Mailbags were dumped on the platform and others were being loaded so we decided it was time to step forward out of the shadows. We glanced left and right, half expecting to be approached by railway police, but a few leaves rustling down the platform were the only movements we saw.

The platform was swathed in a flood of light emanating from the mobile sorting offices. It looked so warm and inviting. The supervisor noticed us standing expectantly in this pool of light, put down his mug of tea, came on the platform and said kindly, 'And what can I do for you lads?' We briefly outlined our plight and before we had finished he enthusiastically welcomed us into his train and in no time at all a much appreciated red-hot cup of tea was thrust into our hands too. The train moved off gently towards Plymouth and it wasn't long before we were fast asleep. Mail sacks make very good mattresses! Three cheers for the Post Office and the Night Mail!

Next morning back onboard the good ship TENBY all the groups met up again recounting their various weekend exploits to a wide variety of destinations. Bold as brass we handed in our folder containing the results of our initiative test and carried on with our normal Monday morning routines. It wasn't long before word filtered back that our researches on Mr Bevan were 'excellent', our rubber stamp from the police station didn't warrant a comment, but as for the life history of the postmistress... that really did cause some consternation in the training office, as apparently it bore virtually no resemblance to the truth. How were we to know that the real postmistress, being the aunt of one of our training staff, had been looking out for us all weekend to welcome us to the valley...?

We told ourselves that we had used our initiative but that wasn't exactly how the training officers saw it! Some suitable minor punishment was handed out but the twinkle in the training staff's eyes indicated we were not about to be thrown out of the Navy. Phew!

Excitement over, we headed off to sea to 'live as sailors live'. I, amongst others, had great difficulty keeping my sense of humour on more than one occasion. On arrival at Portland a group of us were despatched up the mast on a foul Autumn Sunday morning, to scrub and renew the paintwork. Gritting my teeth I kept repeating what they told us at Dartmouth: 'It's all good for the soul,' I muttered as I attempted to revitalise frozen paint splattered fingers. We all agreed that none of us could remember any of this shown in the recruiting adverts.

Shortly after this period I escaped in an unexpected way from this particular luxury cruise with the grey funnel line. Whilst at Devonport I was part of a team entrusted to load piles of weighty frozen food onboard, the incentive being 'as soon as the stores are down below lads you can finish work for the day'. Huge boxes of frozen foods were soon flying about, from dockside across the gangway and down to storerooms deep within the ship. But in my haste something went awry with my lifting technique, my back crumbled, and before anyone could say 'make and mend' I was whisked off to the local naval hospital at Stonehouse.

Doctors prodded, investigated and eventually diagnosed a slipped disc and so I lay between the crisp white sheets of the Officers' Ward whilst my classmates all headed back to sea again. In all honesty I can't say that the ravages of the Pentland Firth in November were preferable to those crisp white sheets and the pretty naval nurses scurrying to and fro…

Youth was on my side so it wasn't long before I was fully fit and back onboard the good ship TENBY. Recalling tales from other Dartmouth cadets about trips to the Mediterranean and Caribbean we plodded round the UK coast, visiting the gorgeous beach of Greenock, followed by the whispering palms along the seafront… at St Ives. The two foreign highlights were to the French naval base at the end of an overnight trip all the way to Brest and the delights of Ghent after a 'cruise' down the Belgian canal system. We were beginning to get used to living the high life!

Despite all the distractions of this 'European cruise' we also managed to do some studies. As the ship returned to Devonport for Christmas we headed back to Dartmouth to face end of term exams with the appropriate amount of trepidation.

During this time we completed a number of Admin duties including being lined up on the beautifully polished quarterdeck at the college to hear of our next appointments to the Fleet. It was a memorable occasion. The same training officer who had told us all that we had no guts, determination or drive after our initiative test to the snow clad lighthouse just months before was about to lecture us again. Now we were being congratulated on a training programme well done etc etc… and then he started reading from a lengthy list outlining the ships to which we as individuals were to be sent for the next part of our training… 'Smith: FISKERTON (Singapore)'… 'Jamieson: CROFTON (Malta)' and much to my surprise 'Critchley STUBBINGTON (Malta)'… he continued on down the list. (It transpired that it had been produced on exam results. I missed the best job by a whisker - the top cadet was the one going off to a minesweeper in far away Singapore, while Malta came second and third on the list.) On and on went the training officer, ending with those who didn't do so well; they were appointed to open bridge minesweepers on Fishery Protection duties around the UK coast. (It is perhaps noteworthy that a former First Sea Lord – the Navy's top officer – was part of that noble group on the Dartmouth quarterdeck that day! He was obviously trained in good company! He was posted to an ancient frigate at Portland.)

Shortly after the Reading of the Great List it was time to party. The annual sparkling end of term Ball was the highlight of the year's social events, as officers' girlfriends headed to South Devon to be whisked around our infamous dance floor. Sadly, those of us who had paid little attention to our dancing instructor (and in any case only knew how to dance like a lady!), or perhaps more to the point hadn't a suitable guest to invite west, were promptly issued with a pair of white gloves. We were to act as car parking attendants albeit in a quite magical setting; flaming torches had been strapped to the trees lining the approach to the college and the hill that night was floodlit. It must have looked like a fairy castle from the other side of the river. Whilst everyone else danced the night away I made a mental note that car parking was not to be my scene when future social events were on the horizon. I would find a girlfriend from somewhere – anywhere – for the next time!

As others concentrated on their correct footwork with the latest lass on their arm my imagination was firmly focussed on my first ship that was waiting for me in the beautiful balmy Mediterranean. Christmas 1963 seemed relentlessly slow in passing; preparations to fly to Malta took on a far higher priority as this very excited eighteen year old prepared to make his personal mark on the long history of the Royal Navy and HMS STUBBINGTON in particular.

CHAPTER FOUR

MALTA BOUND

A bleak, wet January evening - virtually the last day in the UK before our proper seagoing career began - found intrepid travellers Jamieson and Critchley wending their way, fresh out of Dartmouth, through the damp and dreary lanes of Wiltshire in an RAF bus...

The next day, through the windows at RAF Lyneham's departure lounge the gleaming silver Comet 2 waiting for us looked impressive in spite of the downpour and feeble wintry sunlight. We were like young kids off on their first package holiday taking great interest in the sleek early version of the famous Comet jet, at that time in RAF service, which was to whisk us away to the Mediterranean. Ah, the Mediterranean where, of course, the sun always shone...

Soon enough we were on board and our 'adventure' began. Despite having to drop into Nice for fuel to make possible what, in those days, amounted to a long haul flight to Malta we soon exchanged the gale-lashed shores of the UK for the, err, gale-lashed runway of Malta's Luqa airport.

Slithering and sliding along the runway (we were asking ourselves if this pilot had ever flown a Comet before) we were soon on our way after the arrival formalities – customs and immigrations etc. A young Sub Lieutenant, one Jonathan

Drake-Wilkes, who was coming to the end of his time in STUBBINGTON, awaited me at the airport. I was to replace him onboard, releasing him to return to the UK and a new appointment. But before that he had to show me the ropes.

We wound our way through the dimly lit streets of Malta in his very smart, but elderly, cream Sunbeam Talbot sports car, heading for the Msida base where a gaggle of minesweepers awaited us. We spluttered to a halt outside the large corrugated iron gates of the base, gates that looked as if they had seen active service during World War II just twenty years earlier. Maybe they had! Battered and tarnished and squealing their complaints they were eventually eased awkwardly open by a locally recruited MoD Plod (a Ministry of Defence policeman). How he could endure those long nights guarding that heap of scrap metal that doubled as the main gate to the base I'll never know.

Struggling up the gangway with my worldly possessions I was met by a young electrician who I was later told was 'the Spanish dog end' (his surname was Elstub); to my surprise, he helped carry my bags onboard whilst addressing me as 'Sir'. That was definitely a first... I could soon get used to this officer lark! Things had certainly changed since Dartmouth days.

I was then introduced to the entire wardroom staff, being the duty chef plus a steward. I was obviously moving into another, apparently much smaller, world from the one I had just left in the Dartmouth Training Squadron and the after mess deck of HMS TENBY. Before a much-needed sleep I took a wander round my new ship. My first impression was that it was so small – just about the same size as a Gosport ferry from my youth, weighing in at a mere 400 tons. A few small messdecks, the proverbial communications office, three cabins including the Captain's, plus the all-important galley – and that was it.

Thousands of officers and men were trained in these wooden hulled vessels and most of them will warmly recount the genuine fun and companionship of serving in the 'small ship navy', as these Minesweepers were fondly known. The Royal Navy built some 120 Ton class Minesweepers in the 1950's when the Korean War was the focus of planners' attention; this number was far more than history would dictate would be needed in the Fleet so they were subsequently dispatched worldwide for a wide range of other duties.

Formal introductions to the other officers the following day didn't take too long; there were only four of them, including the Captain. He had been a fixed wing navy Sea Hawk pilot before the decision was made that his boots would never touch the pedals of any naval aircraft again. He was however allowed to stay in the Navy when his flying days ended and he was entrusted with the command of this Malta-based Minesweeper. It was soon obvious that his respect by those onboard was at the lower end of the scale although he was loyally supported by 'one of the best' in the shape of the First Lieutenant (Second in Command) one Gerry Couzins. As an experienced ex sailor, he had been promoted to officer rank and it was obvious from day one it was he who kept the whole show together.

One of my jobs was that of Gunnery Officer: we carried a World War II vintage Bofors 40/60 gun on the foc'sle and a similar vintage twin barrelled 20mm Oerlikon weapon located behind the funnel. Apart from that I was delegated two other thrilling roles; those of Correspondence Officer and Supervisor of the ship's canteen fund. My immediate thought was that Nelson had to start somewhere, so if I were eventually to make high command perhaps the canteen fund supervisor was just the place to start!

Our first day at sea was a shock in every sense of the word. It became instantly obvious why travel companies don't send their photographers to the Med in January to capture images for next year's brochures. There were no whispering palms or beautiful blue seas; it was grey, overcast, blustery, with a reasonable swell running. My stomach started to churn.

As I fought back the urge to retire somewhere quiet and think about being sea-sick and sorry for myself, the good ship STUBBINGTON punched her way into the exercise areas off the Maltese coast. I was overjoyed – or do I mean scared rigid – to hear that we were to carry out a gunnery shoot against a real airborne target with a real human being in the aircraft towing the target at the end of a long wire. How on earth would I explain to my Captain that: a) I had no idea whatso-ever what was involved in such an exercise; b) I hadn't the faintest idea what a Gunnery Officer was meant to do or say in such circumstances and moreover; c) could someone get word back to Dartmouth pronto that it may be of more use to train young officers in the delights of small ships' gunnery than the intricacies of ballroom dancing. Totally bemused as to what I should do I wandered off and found a steel helmet; at least I would look the part!

There's probably a Fleet Air Arm wife somewhere who is eternally grateful that in the seconds before her husband over flew a gaggle of bobbing minesweepers in his Meteor Jet I blurted out to my friendly First Lieutenant that I was com-pletely confused, hadn't a clue what I was up to but understood that the pilot of the aircraft rapidly approaching probably expected to survive the exercise. He swiftly stepped into my quaking boots and promptly gave all the correct orders over the ship's communication system. The guns broke out into an impressive display of tracer bullets and, phew, the pilot jetted on to fly another day. At that moment I identified the feeling when a crisis is all over; it is called 'total relief'.

I could breathe again.

So this was life on the ocean waves, Mediterranean style. Mmmmmm…

The next day, thankfully back in harbour in Msida creek, I was introduced to my duties as the ship's Correspondence Officer. I quickly learnt that here was yet another vital skill for which I had been totally unprepared by the experts at Dartmouth; for a start I had no idea how to type. When in harbour my job involved sorting all the official mail for the ship and skilfully distributing it to anyone onboard who could be held vaguely responsible for handling it, and reply-ing. No one had invented the word processor in 1964, so hours of two-finger typ-ing and retyping lay ahead - basic correspondence with blue admiralty pattern carbon paper between the sheets. I was told some of the tricks of the trade by my predecessor before he left, the most interesting one being to find a pretty Wren from the Wrens' accommodation building just yards away at Whitehall Mansions, and persuade her that for a suitable bribe she would love to come onboard and rattle off some correspondence on a very ancient typewriter.

For those of you shocked by the thought of an officer of the RN resorting to extor-tion I ought to explain that there was an unofficial sliding scale of bribery amongst the ships of the Squadron. It ranged from a box of chocolates for a sin-gle letter typed, up to what could be described as the maximum 'service' which deserved at the very least a trip into Valletta for drinks and a meal at The Lantern or some such similar venue. This was because we were usually faced with an almost full sack of mail on the ship's return from what was a normal six-week trip away from Malta.

I was also to learn how to really reduce the load in a small ship's office – which, in effect, was the tiny Minesweeping Office underneath the open bridge – with the tiniest table, plywood desk, filing cabinet and ancient Olivetti typewriter that Samuel Pepys himself had probably used. Here I am, I've done a year's training, and no one has taught me to type or fire weapons.

Moving on to my role as Supervisor of the 'Canteen Fund'... As we were a tiny ship with a modest crew of around twenty-seven and no NAAFI shop onboard, we merely loaded up with beer, soap powder, cigarettes, toothpaste and all the other essentials of life whenever we were at our Maltese base. Once a day a sen-ior rating would open up the Minesweeping store where all these goodies were stored and sell them in a similar fashion to your average village shop. My role was to be responsible for the money, paying the bills and monthly balancing the stock book against the stock held; this I dutifully had to muster down to the last packet of buttons and tins of Johnson's Baby Powder (always a favourite with your roughy-toughie Jack Tar in any warm climate, you will be amused to learn). Again, it was another job for which I was totally untrained and it often flitted through my mind that a week behind the counter of a local Spar would have been more useful than humping a trouser-leg full of wet sand around South Devon during the Dartmouth days – but I mustn't get cynical...

My turnover complete I was the proud owner of a steel helmet for future gunnery shoots, a very inferior typewriter and the keys to the beer and baccy locker. I was ready to start my career as a Midshipman in Her Majesty's Navy. Ready aye ready! I had been told that my duty as one of Her Majesty's naval officers was basically 'to seek out Her Majesty's enemies on the high seas, sink their ships and kill their men.' Reminding myself of this and clutching my keys to the beer locker I waved my predecessor goodbye down the gangway as we parted company, he to the UK and I to the oceans deep. 'Well Critchley – you really are in the Navy now,' I told myself.

Preparations were in hand for our first proper trip. Tony Barber, our navigator, laid a course for Patras in Greece on his charts and we headed out of Msida creek waving to the small clutch of families who gathered along Gzira front to wave their men folk away for a month or so. (In those days if you were married your wife and family went with you to live in a married quarter if you were due to be away from the UK for longer than about 18 months.)

And then it started... wave after wave after wave accosted our little vessel. This was to be no Mediterranean cruise... here was I, a 'proper' officer at last on one of Her Majesty's (albeit tiny) warships having one totally overriding need – to talk to Hughie over the ship's side as I donated my breakfast to any passing needy fish (tinned tomatoes always seemed to feature hugely). We had only been at sea half an hour and here I was heaving my heart out. Knowing that the great Nelson also suffered was no consolation whatsoever... he was dead (just as I wanted to be). Any mal de mer sufferer knows only too well what I am talking about here. Mere words are simply not enough.

Staggering up to the bridge I took over the watch with the Captain lurking in the background to see if I was capable of standing up, let alone standing the four hour Forenoon watch. To this day I have memories of doing my best to keep station on the stern of the Italian tanker STROMBOLI that was taking passage with us to the Greek exercise area. Thankfully navigation was impossible in such poor conditions. One minute our Italian guide could be seen – the next she was lost either down the trough of a wave or in the low visibility shrouding the little gaggle of warships battling against a gale that bleak January day. Oh, how the memories of St Paul's journeys in these waters came back from Sunday school days. He was lucky – at least he got shipwrecked safely and Malta provided him with plenty of terra firma as he stepped ashore at what is now appropriately named St Paul's Bay. We had no choice but to battle on eastwards across the wild Mediterranean. How many days would it all take?

As the journey progressed my watchkeeping didn't. Having deposited my breakfast overboard all was not over as the hours turned into days – or was it weeks - and my seasickness did not relent. I thought my stomach had no lining left. I lay slumped on my bunk watching a steel wastepaper basket roll back and forth as the ship rocked and rolled towards the Greek mainland but I was too weak to do anything about it. Was it day or night? Christmas or Easter? 1850 or 1964? I didn't know – or care. My long-suffering messmates had to share the watches amongst them, as 'the new Mid' was totally incapable. To this day I am so grateful to you chaps!

It's amazing how quickly the stomach recovers – once we hit land I was fine in a jiffy, but the memories remain even after over 40 years.

CHAPTER FIVE

GREEK INTERLUDE

The reason for our long winter haul to Patras (near Athens) was to enable us to take part in one of the many Medsweepex exercises conducted during the sixties, during which Minesweepers from throughout the NATO area assembled to hone their minesweeping skills. The exercises always took place in a different port ranging from one end of the Mediterranean to the other; this time it was the turn of the Greek Navy to be host. The White Ensign had arrived in town, we were ready to sweep any mines that were laid for use; stand by NATO – the Brits are here!

Shortly before the multi national mini-fleet set sail the decision was made that the senior Greek officer embarked in the very ancient (ex UK built) BYMS minesweeper SALAMINIA needed an 'interpreter'. As I had been of little use to the bridge watch-keeping team of STUBBINGTON during the voyage from Malta to Patras you can guess whose name was put forward to act as the new 'interpreter' (and yes, you've guessed - I wasn't taught Greek at Dartmouth either!). As I rapidly packed my bag, a very young (sixteen as opposed to my eighteen, that is) RN Junior Radio Operator, known as Sparks, appeared from somewhere onboard to act as the communication link and we walked down the jetty to join the Greek ship laying at her berth ahead of us just minutes before slipping the berthing ropes.

It was a fine day… at least seasickness wasn't going to be a problem. However, a quick glance at the interior of the Greek ship had us racing back down the jetty to our ship, into the galley and grabbing whatever tinned food we could find. Then there was a mad dash back to the ship seconds before the final berthing ropes were slipped. In hindsight we probably should have deserted at this point.

Re-boarding our new Greek home, we were ushered into the ship's tiny wardroom and told we could sleep where we liked… it was a choice of a bench seat or the deck.

It was not a pleasant sight; it looked as if the shipbreakers had arrived early, and implemented a thousand pounds worth of improvements. Sparks and I went below with our guide and the sight horrified us; frankly it was totally inappropriate for pigs to live in, let alone humans. The health and safety police of the 21st century would have had a field day. It looked as if no one had ever used a bin; all the rubbish, including food, was simply dumped on the deck, strewn throughout the accommodation area. Literally anything would have grown on that composting mess; it was like walking on sponge as you crossed from side to side. A clothes peg (had one been to hand) would have been invaluable for the nose… suddenly I thought I was about to be sick again, but a few gulps of fresh air works wonders.

What on earth had we walked into?

Abandoning my grip with its few clothes and toiletries in the tiny wardroom I headed for the bridge. My duties as the new 'interpreter' were about to start. Was I ever going to do anything in the Royal Navy for which I was even marginally prepared?

Squeezing into the rear of the tiny open bridge minesweeper I visualised those men of an earlier generation of Royal Naval officers watchkeeping on this very bridge in World War II – probably sweeping live mines in the wild North Sea rather than in what was turning out to be quite pleasant Greek, now sheltered, coastal waters.

Spotting the ship's Captain I attempted to introduce myself – there was barely elbowroom to raise an arm to salute him but I made an effort. He was a Lieutenant Commander in the Greek Navy and did actually have a very few words in his English vocabulary. But it was indeed a few… Minutes before sailing the Senior Officer (a Commander) appeared on the bridge. With the CO, the Senior Officer, a Greek communications rating, the 'interpreter' plus his sixteen-year-old junior rating signalman companion the bridge was over full. If anyone wanted to move it had to be into a space created by someone else shifting around – all very cosy!

I attempted to at least pass the time of day with the senior officer, with the help of smiling, saluting and speaking slowly... he seemed to understand my salute but not a single word. As my Greek vocabulary didn't extend much beyond Olympic, Taxi, Coca Cola, Athens and Patras I suspected we were heading for an interesting few days. I would hate to think what skills this eighteen-year-old 'interpreter' would be expected to bring to the exercise!

We headed out towards the exercise area sailing ahead of a huge long line of minesweepers – maybe thirty – as far as the eye could see. It was an impressive sight; mother duck leading her little chicks off to sea. As our diesel engines thumped away below I was unsure what I should do next. While I considered my next move, a conversation between the CO and his Senior Officer close by was becoming more and more heated. There was no escape. I had to remain jammed into a tiny space at the back of the bridge as the decibels got louder and louder. Then as the decibels increased it got physical too as some minor pushing and shoving began beside me.

To this day I have no idea what the argument was about but the climax came as the CO walked to the chart table and picked up the huge Classified NATO operations order outlining every move the ships were planned to make for the next two weeks. This document was some three to four inches thick, and crucial to the exercise. With little or no warning the Operation orders were suddenly airborne heading for the senior officer on the port bridge wing – his face red with rage. I decided that the CO would make a good bowler in any cricket match as I watched him hurl the huge order at his senior officer. He missed his stumps however – and his senior officer. Soon the orders were drifting rapidly away from us astern, fast turning into papier mache – but not a move was made to get any of the ships following in line to recover them.

So... off we headed into the exercise area to take command of NATO's best – without a single order onboard. Someone had doubtless spent months compiling them but it seemed to be of no concern to the officers on the SALAMINIA.

Time to make my escape by squeezing past the warring parties, as I muttered something in English neither of them would have understood. Back to the wardroom below - I was ready for something to eat. Before me was a seaman whom I had seen on deck earlier; he was also to be the steward for this particular cruise of the Greek islands. My eye was transfixed on his blue working shirt and its pattern of patches. I just had to count them – I reckoned there were twenty-seven – some were patches on patches on patches – I wondered if they would count for an entry in the Guinness book of records. These guys were lovely people but very poor.

Although I was ravenous my next worry was that I was going to be offered some kind of food. In the corner of the wardroom was what had once been an iron or steel sink. Its waste pipe had long been removed, the plughole sealed and a gas cylinder and burner positioned below, obviously, in order to heat the contents of the sink. The remnants of the previous evening's meal remained in it – cold and with huge white globules of fat floating like icebergs in the 'stew'. That old familiar feeling of seasickness rapidly came on again and with suitable mutterings I hurried towards the fresh air of the upper deck – for the second time.

How was I going to play this one? My junior radio operator had followed me, and dreaming up a quick medical condition we came up with a plan. A whole heap of excuses were put forward as to why we couldn't eat the Greek offerings, including religion and health. Our hosts were totally unfazed that they didn't have to feed their guests and we were just so relieved. We mustered our nutritional resources liberated from our own ship minutes before sailing. It totalled two large tins of Herrings in Tomato Sauce – an old Navy favourite – and six small tins of cherries. They were destined to last us four or five days but we had no complaints whatsoever as we found a corner in the fresh air on the upper deck to eat our supper!

As the exercise somehow or other swung into action, sweep-wires were fed out over the stern and the long, frequently boring, minesweeping routine commenced. Minesweeping laps were swept again and swept again. (A minesweeper acts very much like a farmer ploughing his fields traversing up and down the field moving further towards the extremity as he progresses. A minesweeper marks out a sea 'field' and then tows a variety of sweeps through the field to sweep or detonate any deadly mine within its operating area.)

After a period of some basic wire sweeping just to ascertain if any moored mines of ancient – but still deadly – vintage had been laid it was time to recover the wire sweeps, stream 'the loop' and start looking for magnetic mines (these are mines that explode when a large magnetic field, such as a ship, passes by). The loop consisted of a huge cable made of cork (to keep it afloat) but with a heavy-duty copper cable running through it; this took a large current, which created a magnetic field far greater than the minesweeper itself produced. A pulse generator onboard specifically produced a huge current to be passed down the loop. Once the loop itself was streamed four brass lugs at the inboard end of the cable had to be inserted into a junction box and four bolts tightened to keep the lugs in place. It was then time to start the pulse generator, to get into the minefield and start the laps as the loop became live – and a magnetic field established. Frequently a mine would be fitted with a device that counted a pre-set number of magnetic fields that passed before exploding. A simple transit of the lap was never good enough – it had to be done once and then over and over again. Frequently boring but we were told, essential stuff!

As the sun dipped behind the beautiful Aegean islands all around us it was time to sneak off and share a whole tin of cherries with my fellow Brit before retiring for the night – leaving my fellow NATO comrades to be responsible for the ship as it headed back and forth up and down the laps. When the wardroom was empty and 'Patch' the steward had cleared away I made my way to find my sleeping bag to spend my first night onboard. I had done little interpreting to earn my keep but it was all part of the training I kept telling myself. Good for the soul, didn't they tell us as Dartmouth?

Slipping into my sleeping bag after a trip to the Heads – the toilet (I'll spare you the details) I settled down to sleep on the bare deck with about fourteen tinned cherries in my stomach giving me the familiar feeling of wellbeing that follows a memorable meal – well, almost. All outside was absolutely calm as the ship ploughed up a lap; however, as it turned through 180 degrees at the end of each lap it rolled gently and it was then that I noticed what could best be described as a 'little local difficulty'. When the ship rolled to port the wooden door leading on to the upper deck closed (the lock had long since 'gone missing'), filling its frame before it gently swung open again. When the ship turned to starboard however the door swung towards its frame but was unable to fill the gap. The whole of the wooden superstructure of the ship was shifting slightly and not allowing the door to fill its frame. It didn't need a naval architect to realised something wasn't quite right! I had seen enough for the first day. As the interpreter I had none of the watch-keeping duties my fellow officers just a few hundred yards away on the STUBBINGTON could look forward to, so I was soon asleep – and 'all night in' too. A rare treat.

Early next morning I congratulated myself that I had indeed slept through the drone of the pulse generators; with the sun streaming into the tiny wardroom it was time to get up and savour the view. On the horizon I could see a cruise liner 'doing' the islands. I bet their passengers ate better fare than a few tinned cherries last night, I mused, but I had to distract my mind from such things… Soon dressed, I went for a wander on the upper deck to take the air. It was just one of those sunrises where you have to thank your Maker that you were up and about to witness such a sight. Simply Wonderful!

Taking the first lung full of mild Mediterranean morning air my wanderings took me past the huge junction box where the loop was inserted – or had been bolted.

43

Whoever had secured the lugs into the box… hadn't. Two of the four lugs simply dangled from the cable – there wasn't a single amp going down the huge loop streamed behind us – and probably hadn't been all night. I went to the bridge and in Midshipman sign language managed to get my message over that all was not well on the sweep deck. A sailor, about to light up his morning fag, put the cigarette behind his ear, clambered down from the bridge and sauntered down to the sweep deck to find out what the problem was.

It was soon obvious exactly what the problem was… but his priority was to light his first fag of the day. It looked as if it was a cigarette paper filled with sweepings from the deck. He must have been short of matches so he simply took one of the lugs (fortunately lightly insulated where he placed his hands) and arced it against the metalwork of the junction box. The subsequent arcing he produced was good enough to provide part of any municipal firework display – blue lightening seemed to be streaking everywhere. I stood well back as he arced his lug against the junction box yet again, whilst leaning well forward with the cigarette in his mouth. Despite the pyrotechnics round about him somehow or other he lit his cigarette at the first attempt, without killing himself. Miracles never cease!

Once the cigarette was lit he could worry about getting the loop back into an operational state. Eventually other men arrived on the upper deck wiping sleep from their eyes and – after much rising of Greek voices – decided the way forward. Half an hour later the ship was operational once again, the generator having been shut down, cables fixed – properly – and then the generator coaxed back into life.

Later…after the altercations of the previous day I swapped stories with Sparks as we took the air on deck and wandered back to the bridge. The hours ticked by as we ploughed up and down many a lap on our minesweeping routine, and the weak winter sun really was quite pleasant on the back of my neck; far better in these enclosed waters off Patras than tackling the wild seas off Malta – was that nightmare really only a week behind me? The atmosphere was much more settled today and it seemed an appropriate time to attempt a conversation with the Captain as he, unshaven, made light work of something on a plate that may have been described as his breakfast. By pointing at the sun, smiling and saying slowly 'Nice day' I was actually communicating though it could hardly be described as 'interpreting'.

'When… the… exercise… is… over… Captain,' I started, 'where… will… you… go?' expecting him to indicate that he would be returning to a local naval base… or into dry dock perhaps? I was somewhat taken aback when he simply replied, 'Prison!'

I wanted to keep the conversation going but how does an eighteen-year-old very junior RN officer take the conversation from there with a fellow NATO officer old enough to be his father? 'I... am... sorry... to... hear... that... Sir,' was the best I could come out with, but he seemed quite happy to tell me, as far as he was able in his halting English, the sad tale and the reason for his forthcoming incarceration. If Greek warships were bad enough, with their grim domestic facilities and lacklustre approach to most things technical, what would one of their military prisons be like, I mused?

It transpired that a few months before the exercise he had married his fiancée and such were the appallingly low salaries in the Greek forces at the time that his options for a honeymoon destination were strictly limited, if not non existent (my young signalman worked out that as a sixteen-year-old he was earning more in his RN pay packet in a week than this poor Greek Lieutenant Commander earned in a month). He obviously wanted to give his lady the decent honeymoon I'm sure she deserved but was very severely strapped for cash. Inspiration obviously came in a flash... as the captain of a minesweeper why not use the fine vessel he had been entrusted to command and take his wife off for a wonderfully romantic sea cruise?

So... he married, embarked his brand new wife, and without telling a single soul set off on his honeymoon cruise. He recounted that when the Admiral totted up his minesweepers in harbour the next day he was doubtless none too pleased that one seemed to be missing. Without a care in the world the Lieutenant Commander headed off for his honeymoon cruise. Corfu, he decided, would be pleasant at this time of the year – so he set course towards Corfu, again without telling a soul.

Despite the time it took to relate the long story in pidgin Anglo-Greek an intriguing tale unfolded as the minesweeper ploughed its furrow through the exercise area hour after hour.

'And... what... happened... next?' Seemingly he and his new wife enjoyed their cruise up the western seaboard of the Greek coast heading for Corfu Town just a few miles from the hostile Albanian shores. Not a soul had spotted him as he and his men cruised the tranquil waters of the Aegean Sea, though the crew probably did wonder what was going on! I had a slight feeling that the Operations room of his local naval Headquarters would not have been as calm as he recounted, as word spread ashore that 'one of our minesweepers is missing!'

Our enterprising newlyweds made it to Corfu and even as he settled into his honeymoon on the beautiful island no one ashore seemed to consider that a minesweeper anchored in the harbour was worth reporting to Athens. Such ships frequently called; no one in the harbour office – or anyone else – ever reported the matter to a higher authority. Why should they? It all seemed totally routine.

As the days ticked by and Admirals were still one minesweeper short in their fleet more and more drastic measures were taken to try and find the missing vessel. No doubt the seas were searched in an ever-widening arc from the base, and as radio messages went unanswered questions would have been raised as to whether the vessel was even still afloat. Inter-service rivalries were put to one side – in spite of red faces – the Air Force were called in to scour the seas. Eventually, to senior officers relief, the missing SALAMINIA was found, quietly lying at anchor in Corfu harbour, by a flying boat, which landed close by. The aircrew arrested the romantic Captain… and the honeymoon was over.

I was not surprised to hear that a Court Martial followed and a prison sentence deemed appropriate for the run away commander. However… the NATO exercise was looming and the SALAMINIA was scheduled to be part of it. With a dearth of Minesweeper Captains, the Greek Naval authorities had no alternative but to delay the departure of my new captain to the local prison; the exercise was of more importance than the prison sentence so he kept his command and he could look forward to meeting the man with the cell keys once the exercise was over.

It was an interesting tale for a wide-eyed, impressionable young Midshipman. As the minesweeping continued I dared to say, 'and… when… does… the… new… Captain… arrive… to… take… command… of… this… ship?' I should have guessed; the Greek Navy were so short of minesweeper CO's not only did they have to use this captain for the current exercise, but when he did finally serve his time in prison they would have to keep the ship in harbour for the duration of his sentence. No one was available to fill his shoes – there was no alternative or back-up!

The morning's conversation, albeit haltingly slow, had been fascinating; it was time to find Sparks – he had the key to his suitcase and in it the can of 'herrings in tomato sauce' we had promised ourselves. It was all we were likely to eat that day… or could we allocate ourselves the luxury of another tin of cherries – to share? I was getting very hungry but the thought of those fatty icebergs languishing in the sink were more than enough to keep me away from whatever food was on offer. And so it went on. Day followed day – as did our empty tins over the ship's side.

The other abiding memory of minesweeping Greek style was that of secure communications. When the vessel was built the requirement for a secure communications system simply didn't exist but twenty years on times had changed. As a NATO vessel the SALAMINIA was required to carry the same crypto encoding equipment as much larger vessels. The NATO SECRET key cards had to be kept in a safe, mustered each day by an officer until used (for just twenty-four hours on their appointed day) in the secret encrypting device. Should one of these cards end up in the wrong hands the whole of the NATO communications system was in danger of being totally compromised for up to one month.

In the Royal Navy the custody of these cards was taken very seriously indeed. The Greek Navy, lacking the space to house this equipment, appeared simply to have gone to their nearest garden centre, purchased a conventional garden shed and had it strapped to the deck of their minesweepers with two large iron bands over the top to prevent it being blown overboard. They were thus in business with a 'Communications Centre.'

There seemed to be no restrictions as to who had access to the garden shed – myself, an unknown visitor, included. On entering 'the shed' with the wind in the wrong direction there was every chance that at least two or three of these highly secret A5 sized folded key cards would be sucked out and deposited overboard in their smart plastic wallets. It certainly happened – the shed was frequently open to the elements and the cards sucked out. They never seemed to be kept in the ship's safe as NATO regulations insisted…

At last the order was given for the SALAMINIA to have a twelve-hour stand down back in harbour. We were going 'home', back to Patras. No one had indicated that my interpreting role was over but, had anyone on my own ship suggested that I was to return to the Greek vessel, they would have had a mutiny on their hands.

We scurried back to our own ship once it too had entered harbour for a stand down period. Without waiting for the ship to be properly secured we were determined to reach the galley in the shortest time possible; never has a bacon sandwich tasted so good. Sea sickness… fatty Greek icebergs… three cheers for the life-saving qualities of tinned cherries I said to my messmates as I turned into my 'proper' bunk with clean sheets that night, behind a door that fitted into the hole the builders had successfully built for it in my cabin too… wonderful!

Back in Malta after my first Medsweepex it was time to put into practice a few tricks of the trade as far as my duties as the ship's Correspondence Officer were concerned. As we had been away from our Maltese base for four or five weeks the mail had built up. Our signalman was also the 'postie' and everyone was delighted to see him staggering down the jetty with a sack of mail rather than his normal daily handful when in Malta; everyone that is except the Correspondence Officer!

As the others concentrated on getting ashore to their families the poor old 'Corr O' had to get to work on what was left in the mail sack once all the personal mail had been removed and distributed. At least 50% of the contents remained: discarding a stack of mail in brown envelopes that looked neither interesting or important helped reduce the pile by about 20%, but what, I mused, was I to do with the remainder... the chart corrections (always for the North Sea I told myself – totally irrelevant to where we were – a chart needs changing so send a chart to every ship in the world), notifications of NAAFI price increases and other similarly scintillating envelopes. I worked out a solution, bundled them up and placed them in the sack in which they had been flown out from London. I then addressed the label to myself onboard HMS STUBBINGTON – but care of the Resident Naval Officer in Bermuda – and by Sea Mail. The role of the Fleet mail office was simply to direct their sacks to wherever the label indicated, not to query any labels. Easy!

So, as I went ashore intent on rapidly developing my badly neglected social life, with the minimum of paperwork behind me, the bulk of our mail headed for Bermuda – by sea- via London. This was my reasoning... if there was something in the mail that was important someone would send a signal to chase up a reply (it wasn't my job to answer signals). If it wasn't important I deduced that it was a good job I had sent it off on a world cruise, rather than waste my time on matters unimportant (I'm not sure my thinking quite complied with official regulations). I always wondered why the naval postman in Bermuda didn't question the fact that he got half a sack of mail for a small, unidentified, minesweeper about every six weeks. He simply re-addressed it 'unknown' back to London who in turn readdressed it back to Malta. The system worked and kept the paperwork to a minimum – no problem, and let me nicely off the hook as far as work was concerned. No one ever rumbled my system.

CHAPTER SIX

BACK TO ENGLAND

As the summer arrived the Mediterranean flattened out, and our trips away on Medsweepex exercises became much more pleasurable than that first sortie to Patras. We roamed the Med from the Turkish port of Izmir in the east to Gibraltar in the west, exercising with our NATO partners whilst taking time off to view more cities and villages than the average teenager in England would ever have had an opportunity to visit. It was at a time when the recruiters could genuinely claim one could 'Join the Navy and see the world.' The fantastic remains of Ephesus were explored in Turkey… and the streets of Thessalonica welcomed us as we trod in the footsteps of the Apostle Paul two thousand years earlier.

Minesweeping for ten days off the French Isle de Levant, in the western Mediterranean, with its extensive nudist colony was probably a mistake by those who plan these things (the binoculars were a highly popular item of equipment at this point). Climbing to the top of the rock of Gibraltar was another experience much enjoyed. All came within weeks of each other.

Whilst at Gibraltar in STUBBINGTON I was informed that I was to join a survey ship for 'astro navigational training', a box I had to tick to become a qualified Officer of the Watch. In no time I had packed and found myself walking round the large dry docks at Gibraltar and up the gangway of the white painted survey ship VIDAL; she was in port to take on fuel and stores at the end of her survey season in the Atlantic. I was on board to understudy the ship's navigator, Geoff Hope. The ship's kindly super qualified surveyor had to instil the mysteries of Astro navigation to this Midshipman. Basic navigation was difficult enough to take in but Astro navigation was much more daunting. We had learnt a very few basics at Dartmouth a year earlier and now I would be putting these into practise. The task was straightforward enough; I simply had to navigate (under supervision of course) this particular vessel from Gibraltar to Portsmouth using only the stars in the heavens above!

Each day two hours before sunrise for five days or so I scrambled out of my bunk in the dark and, armed with a sextant, an accurate timepiece, a copy of the nautical almanac and reams of blank paper, listened intently as my instructor, doubtless overjoyed to be up at that time of day solely for my benefit, tried to instil the art of 'Astro' in me. I found it mind-blowing to star gaze, to identify those stars in the heavens above that I had selected for my calculations the night before. It felt primeval when I was younger, but to this day I am still amazed that by taking a simple angle of a star in the heavens, visually bringing it down to the horizon by use of the sextant, and then recording the time accurately the almanac could be used to calculate both latitude and longitude.

I still consider Astro a 'black art' not fully understood by this Midshipman – but it obviously works and history does recount that the good ship VIDAL made it back to the Solent on time without any undue mishaps. I felt ten feet tall as we approached the coast and the Isle of Wight ferries came into view. I like to tell myself that it was all my own work – with only just a little help from the professionals.

I was duly awarded my 'Astro Nav certificate', one of the many pieces of paper I needed to fully qualify as a seaman officer in the Royal Navy.

One particular night shortly before we reached Portsmouth is etched forever in my memory. After months of surveying in the Atlantic Ocean vast quantities of data had been obtained and a percentage of them used to draw a draft chart of the seabed, by hand, that had been particularly intensely surveyed. It was a beautiful work of art representing weeks and weeks of work undertaken in all weathers. Royal Naval Hydrographic service traditions dictated that before entering harbour at the end of a season the beautiful chart would be taped over the wardroom table then covered with a sturdy sheet of polythene and a full mess dinner held with the work of many months acting as the tablecloth, below the silverware on the gently rocking table.

As the new boy onboard and hardly a member of the mess I was 'volunteered' to act as the Second Officer of the Watch from 2000 to midnight whilst the rest of the wardroom enjoyed one of their last meals together of that particular survey-ing season, the first officer of the watch putting in the odd appearance too when all was quiet on the bridge. I knew that the normally strictly enforced 'no drink-ing at sea' rule was likely to be relaxed slightly that night, and as we were delib-erately well outside the shipping lanes even a Midshipman could hold the fort on the bridge for a while.

The watch was no problem as the miles to Portsmouth steadily reduced, until well after midnight when I went to check that the helicopter pilot who would be responsible for the dreaded Middle watch (from midnight to 0400) was indeed up and about – but just running late.

What I found was a highly entertaining spectacle. He was up, but only just! I dis-covered him in the passageway outside his cabin. He had changed into his flying overalls so it seemed that he had intended to carry out his watch, but his general demeanour indicated that meanwhile he had obviously been dragged into the wardroom celebrations (kicking and screaming I'm sure) and appeared to have 'partaken of adult beverages'.

I could only imagine that the following had happened: for some reason before heading for the bridge he had returned to his cabin, perhaps to collect something. On sliding back the aluminium door he could see the contents of his cabin – sink, chair, bunk, wardrobe etc. But as he stepped into his personal space an unseen hand instantly threw him out again. Picking himself up – literally – from the pas-sageway – he attempted to regain entry to the cabin. Again he failed as within a micro second of stepping over the sill of the doorway he was once again back on the deck in the passage way.

By the time I appeared on the scene he was completely confused. I hid as best I could behind a fire extinguisher to watch the fast developing saga unfold. I was not alone – other officers from the party were in the area trying to melt into the bulkheads with the Atlantic Ocean outside rushing past as the ship headed north.

After the third failed attempt our pilot friend stepped back a few paces, gathered up all the energy he could muster, and literally threw himself at his cabin, with exactly the same result.

By now, to those of us who gathered outside the cabin, it was perfectly obvious what was going on. A so-called friend had placed one of the ship's huge Met balloons (normally used to whisk weather reporting instrumentation into the upper atmosphere) in the cabin and, using a bottle of gas, fully inflated it before closing the door. The thin clear polythene of the huge balloon had moulded itself round all the contents of the cabin...

Finally our gallant pilot realised what was going on. Stitched onto the lower leg of his flying overalls was a sizeable knife (standard equipment for the day he might find himself entangled in the cords of his parachute). With the knife raised to shoulder height he threw himself at the balloon. It was no contest – the knife won and within seconds he found himself hitting the deck, successfully in his cabin this time, surrounded, of course, by vast quantities of a fast deflating weather balloon.

Task completed, he fell asleep in the debris of his balloon whilst someone else trudged up to the bridge to carry out the watch. It doubtless cost the pilot dearly at a later date...

Happy days!

CHAPTER SEVEN

MALTESE INDEPENDENCE

My feet hardly touched the ground once VIDAL was safely back in Portsmouth. Faster than you could say 'Sliema sea front' I was on a plane and whisked back to Malta, my Astro navigation certificate in my rucksack. I had no idea what my role would be this time; maybe I was needed to count the stock of the canteen again or type some more wretched letters.

This was 1964 and the days when Malta was heading for independence, so troop numbers were being reduced. Some ships were even being withdrawn. The Union Jack ashore was about to be lowered for the last time, although it was agreed between the two governments that some troops and ships would remain on a limited basis.

Before they left for the UK for the last time the last two remaining submarines of the World War II much-famed 10th Squadron were carrying out final exercises from the Msida base from just ahead of the minesweeper's berth. When in port, the Wrens at Whitehall Mansions just yards away were frequently complaining that their privacy was being invaded by bored submariners taking a great interest in using the boat's periscopes right outside their quarters at the end of the working day. Yes, perhaps it was time for them to move on...

The decision had been taken in the sixties that the Royal Navy were to build huge nuclear powered submarines to take the Polaris missile system to sea when the RAF handed over their nuclear strike role to the Navy. So, the hunt was on for suitable officers and men to serve as volunteers on board these huge vessels then being designed. You may recall that my Dartmouth class had already been introduced to the delights of the submarine escape tank at Gosport within days of joining the Navy. Now there was going to be another attempt to get a few more young volunteers for the submarine service. I was to spend a week at sea in the ancient T class submarine THERMOPYLAE – built in the dark days between 1943 and 1945 – exercising off the Maltese coast, above and below the surface.

Like other submarine visitors before and after me I was taken right forward on reporting onboard to the torpedo compartment right in the bow. Here, a dozen or so torpedoes lay on their racks ready for instant use in the tubes that lay ahead of me. My bed was to be between two torpedoes rolled together with something that was meant to be a slim mattress on top of them (there was no way I would roll out in a rough sea) and I certainly wasn't encouraged to think about the vast quantities of high explosive inches below my body.

Watch keeping on the tiny submarine bridge was interesting; I idly watched the seas slop over the saddle tanks as the watch progressed while we pushed our way along on the surface. On asking for permission to scramble down into the pressure hull below to answer the call of nature I was told that such a trip was unnecessary as a tube was provided on the small bridge forward of the fin. Doing what had to be done was easy and the resultant liquid would trickle down onto the saddle tanks and off into the sea. There was also another tube on the bridge that was for communicating between the bridge and chart table in the pressure hull below. I am embarrassed to relate that I used the wrong tube; the chart and a jacket that someone had left in the wrong place far below received an unexpected watering…it was all part of the learning curve I kept hearing about.

We slipped below the surface, a new and fascinating experience. It became a little unnerving as the deeper we went the pressure on the hull resulted in audible cracks when the rivets in the pretty ancient submarine took the strain of the external water pressure.

Before I left the boat at the end of my week's 'aquatint' visit, clutching my dirty washing, I remade up my mind I had no desire whatsoever to join the noble band of RN submariners despite all the efforts made to spark some form of interest.

Following this I was dispatched to a fine Daring class destroyer for a week to broaden my experience as a Midshipman. I joined the DIAMOND lying at buoys in Dockyard creek on a quiet Sunday evening. It was a magical experience resting on my bunk on a hot summer evening with all the typical Maltese smells drifting off from the shore as the wake from passing boats lapped gently against the ship's side just a few feet below the open porthole in the cabin.

A week was spent at sea spending most of my time going round the various departments onboard to acquaint myself with a different navy on these "big ships"- and the crew always found a few dirty jobs for the Mid to do too! Two other midshipmen were also under training onboard – one a Nigerian had the almost English surname of Knight - handy for a Mid (Midshipman) to be known as Mid Knight. His chum from Ghana however had a totally unpronounceable name but naturally became Mid 2359 throughout his time onboard. They both thought it a huge joke. (I met one of them years later but he was still calling himself Lieutenant 2359 - even after promotion.)

We returned from our week of sea training – firing the guns ...chasing submarines and the like to lie alongside the ancient hull of the huge repair ship AUSONIA, which had dominated the Gzira skyline for many years. She too was preparing to leave her creek by the shore base HMS PHOENICIA for the last time and head back to England; her service in Malta was over and the scrapyard beckoned.

Soon it was time to prepare for the Independence Day celebrations. The plan for the big day, as far as the minesweepers were concerned, was for them to proceed from their Msida base out to sea for a few miles as the sun set, and then rig aluminium poles over the starboard side of the ships with huge lamps and all the necessary fittings to direct the light to illuminate the ship's structure at the appointed moment on return to harbour. The result should have been a ship totally illuminated. It had worked well in harbour the previous day and looked superb!

In total darkness the five minesweepers turned to reverse their tracks when a mile offshore to then enter the Grand Harbour with excited Maltese residents using every vantage point to view our part of the spectacle.
.

They headed to the 'switch on position' off the Custom's House steps. No one onboard had noticed however that as the ships made their turn at sea to prepare for their run into harbour all the 'illuminating poles – lights for the use of' had fallen off their temporary brackets and were trailing alongside the ships' hulls. As stop watches ticked by to get the ships to the right place at the right time it was a case of a 5...4...3...2...1... 'Switch on' as all the ships' communicators passed the instructions over the radio circuits. Eventually the instructions came.

The ships were indeed in the right place at the right time but as the command came over the airwaves the high power lights were indeed switched on as planned. They were all pointing at every conceivable angle however... some were even underwater... so, instead of the mass of spectators ashore in the Upper Barakka gardens being treated to the sudden illumination of five ships in the darkness, they saw a 'modern futuristic' display as the arts community would doubtless describe the long planned display of lights pointing in every direction.

It was at that time that the huge repair ship AUSONIA made her final trip to sea – a requirement for her in order to retain duty free cigarette and drinks privileges onboard. The normal procedure was for her to make a ten-day trip away to Sicily or Crete, much to the chagrin of many of the families who were used to their men folk returning home most nights. We Midshipmen considered it would be a bit of innocent fun to don a sailor's uniform each, complete with a cap and AUSONIA cap tally and visit a few establishments along the Sliema front. There seemed to be a great rush for the door by some ladies as we entered – they obviously suddenly considered they should really be elsewhere as their men folk had obviously come home early! I suppose it was the sort of thing Midshipmen find funny.

CHAPTER EIGHT

SICILY TOO

Less than a hundred miles to the north of Malta lay Sicily, a frequently scheduled island visit for the Malta based minesweepers. My first Sicilian experience was a visit to Catania on the east coast, an easy overnight trip from Malta.

Before any HM ship arrives in any foreign port a signal is sent in advance to the local British embassy or consulate. Known as a 'Logreq' (Logistic Requirement) on it, a ship's captain can ask for any requirements for his vessel he would like the shore authorities to meet; fuel, food, official calls, shore power supplies – literally anything to make a visit run smoothly and to enable his vessel to return to sea again in a fully operational condition.

For the Catania visit a simple one-line request had been added to the Logreq signal: 'a game of football would be appreciated'.

On entering harbour in the early morning soft light with the volcano Etna rumbling away as a backdrop, we were met by an immaculately attired swarthy Lieutenant of the Italian Navy. He proudly announced that all the requests made in the Logreq had been or would be met and added, 'By the way, the football will be on Thursday afternoon at 2pm – I'll send a bus for the team and supporters,' as he swept ashore.

In a Minesweeper with a crew of just twenty seven men, five or six of whom were required to form a 'duty watch' and could thus not step ashore for the twenty four hours of their duty, the process known in football circles as 'team selection' was not one that concerned the team manager too much. Eventually, and somewhat hastily, eleven men found themselves selected. A rummage through the sports locker revealed enough shirts and shorts (in three different colours) to kit out a team and off they went by bus to discover what sort of team the local Italian Lieutenant had been able to fix for a friendly game. There was a light-hearted atmosphere on the bus; a much-appreciated afternoon off the ship for a quick knock-about was a popular distraction for the crew...

As the bus left the town a huge football stadium eventually came into sight – it must have been at least half the size of our Wembley stadium back at home. The bus came to a halt and we remarked that they had even gone to the trouble of flying the Union Jack from the stadium flagpoles high above us. Eleven players, four supporters, and the ship's dog (an Alsatian called Chokka on temporary loan from another vessel for a few weeks) gingerly left the bus. As we walked towards the stadium the penny dropped... big time! We had expected a small knock-about on any old patch of flat ground with a few piles of crumpled sweaters as goal posts. We found ourselves at the largest stadium on the island where we were to be pitted against a combined Italian armed forces team who just happened to be touring Sicily at that time. There was a definite worried look all round as our players headed for the palatial dressing rooms, while our supporters (all four of us) were led by our Italian hosts to our appointed seats by the pitch.

As we gazed around and took in the fact that the Italians had managed to produce at least five hundred supporters, stories of Christians being thrown to the lions came to my mind. It was obvious our shouts of encouragement or tactical advice were going to pass unheard as the Italians tuned their voices.

To relax us before the start of the game our hosts had laid on some gentle background music – nothing less than a huge fifty-piece band of air force musicians. Immaculately turned out in smart blue uniforms with white sashes they cut a dashing sight as they marched onto the pitch to take up their position centre stage. Shortly afterwards our boys entered the 'arena' to a passable rendering of our national anthem. A quick glance in their direction told me that they were 'somewhat concerned' – to say the least!

The band had come from mainland Italy for a tour of their own, so it was obvious that we were in for a longer musical introduction to the match than just a couple of national anthems. Off went the band to one end of the pitch where they commenced a lengthy programme of marching and counter marching up, across and then back again. The pitch was so large I swear you could see the curvature of the earth.

Were my eyes deceiving me as they marched past for the third time? No, I was right… a flute player almost at the back who was not required to play throughout each piece had actually lit up a cigarette for a quick drag when not playing! It was quite a sight to see him play with a lit cigarette behind his ear when he was musically occupied but when he had a few bars of other non-flute music in his score he would take a surreptitious drag on his fag and then bring hand and cigarette down to his side whilst he exhaled – all the time keeping in good step with his other bandsmen. He had it off to a fine art, the cigarette back behind his ear when it was the time for the flute to join in the melody again! Once we had spotted the secret smoker we couldn't take our eyes off him – we knew we would never see anything like it on Horseguards parade, or anything similar, so we just had to savour the moment!

Eventually the music stopped and it was time for the game. Our team in their rainbow coloured strip received a tumultuous welcome from the Italian supporters; surely they were descendants of the mob who cheered at the Coliseum hundreds of years before…

As the game got underway the ball soon started to find its way into the back of the net as slick Italian footballers passed it with so little effort amongst each other, hardly necessitating their moving across the beautifully manicured grass. Our boys, however, seemed to be doing nothing other than racing from one end of the pitch to the other as a pack of them chased the ball – all of them shouting tactical advice to each other – constantly!

Within the first ten minutes of the game those of us packed into the British supporters area suspected we were about to watch the complete whitewash of our team. But maybe all was not lost as, unbeknown to us, the secret weapon, an unusual substitute, was about to join the team. Remember Chokka? Well, he obviously detected a voice he recognised and with no warning whatsoever he was off like a rocket into the centre of the pitch. On satisfying himself which of the motley crew panting away was the one he knew he was immediately diverted by the ball passing close by. Off he went in the direction of the ball. The Italians played on, awaiting the whistle that never came, so we on the benches were entertained as the Italians kicked the ball with great verve from one to another whilst a seemingly wild Alsatian – ears laid flat back – raced from player to player only to realise that the ball had left seconds earlier… so on he would rush to the next player. The sight warranted a scene in a Disney film; it turned out to be the one light moment in what was destined to be a very serious international 'friendly' being played out before our eyes.

Chokka was eventually securely restrained to the security barriers and we settled down to watch goal after goal being scored against our heroes. We soon gave up making valiant excuses as why each goal was a fluke… a lucky pass… snatched behind the eyes of a biased ref, etc etc etc… The score sheet became irrelevant but the fact that eleven semi-fit sailors managed to chase the ball for two complete halves of the match was nothing less than amazing – a credit to the senior service if not Her Majesty herself. Only one of the team had to be escorted off the pitch briefly after he had deposited his tot of rum (issued to the whole team just hours before the game) mixed with his lunch on the beautifully manicured grass. Perhaps it was the rum that indeed had kept them all going for so long?

Having recovered from the strain of the football match a group of us decided it was time to savour the high life. Ian Henderson, myself and a young Royal Fleet Auxiliary officer who had scrounged a ride with us to Sicily while his ship was in dry dock decided we were going to 'do' the smart and beautiful resort of Taormina. We could just about afford to hire the smallest Fiat car going and all squeezed in to head off north – no hotel or anything pre-booked.

On arriving at the beautiful resort after a pleasant drive we were mightily impressed. Which hotel would we check into? Which restaurant would we honour with our custom? Would we go to the opera or casino that evening? Questions… questions…questions… When we dug deep into our pockets and pooled our finances the bottom line was that we could only just about afford the car parking fee for our tiny Fiat 500 and certainly not a room in one of the fine hotels that overlooked the bay sparkling below us.

So, having wandered around the streets aimlessly…glancing in some very acceptable restaurants frequented by some very beautiful Sicilian ladies we ended up with a total purchase of three postcards, one for each of our respective mums back in England, and headed out of town to find a suitable and free parking lot – what else was there to do? We were obviously all going to have to sleep in our tiny tiny hire car!

We had to spend the night in the town because driving back to the ship with our tails between our legs was more than we could contemplate; we needed to return at least with the illusion of having had a good time. Facing a night in the car was not exactly the high life we had pictured when we started out but needs obviously must… We stretched out as best we could and somehow or other we managed to drop off.

Shortly after 3am the sleeping beauty on the miniscule back shelf masquerading for a seat woke up in great panic. Someone outside had lit a match and was peering into the car, the view severely hindered by the condensation that had built up during our time asleep. Not only was our onlooker a frightening sight, the light from the match also revealed he was holding a .38 pistol against the glass of the passenger window!

Never in the history of Formula One motor racing has a key been put into an ignition… turned… and a car raced off from the grid to the squealing of tyres as happened to our little Fiat that night. Whatever was going on we were well pleased to be clear of it. Eventually we found another parking lot, grabbed a few more hours' shut-eye and eventually made our way back to the ship with all sorts of totally untrue stories of a wild weekend away.

CHAPTER NINE

DOCTOR AT SEA

All ships need to stop to carry out maintenance and repairs – but it's not the same for Midshipmen who, it seemed, must be employed twenty-four hours a day, seven days a week.

When STUBBINGTON was programmed to enter dry dock it was decided that, rather than take a few well-earned days' rest, I would go off to a Royal Fleet Auxiliary (RFA) vessel to see how they operated and gain yet more insight into the many facets of naval life.

The RFA service is part of the Ministry of Defence using theoretically civilian Merchant Navy ships, although in apparel they are painted grey just like any war-ship. Manned by civilians, they function as stores ships and tankers, following the Navy wherever it goes to provide the vessels and personnel with all their needs from fuel, ammunition and spare parts to food and essential supplies. They are literally a combined floating supermarket and warehouse.

At that time, the somewhat antiquated 8,000ton RFA WAVE RULER was the tanker attached to the Med Fleet. Based in Malta she had a crew of UK officers and Maltese ratings.

After bobbing around the Med in a tiny Minesweeper it was great to be onboard a 'proper' ship that wasn't going to bob anywhere as we were slowly eased by tugs from our berth in Grand Harbour for a short spell at sea.

That particular week onboard I moved from department to department taking a close look at how they ticked. Being 'employed' however the department head saw fit meant that I usually found myself tackling a dirty job the staff had been putting off for weeks. More often that not I found myself in some obscure compartment wearing a grubby old pair of overalls. 'Good for the soul,' was the cry I reminded myself again from days at Dartmouth as I cleaned floors, chipped paint, cleaned bilges and washed bulkheads on this World War II veteran still serving.

WAVE RULER spent a fair proportion of her life alongside Parlatorio wharf in Malta, only proceeding to sea when a British or perhaps NATO warship needed to be supplied with fuel somewhere in the Mediterranean. For a first time observer replenishment at sea (RAS in Navy jargon) is quite an interesting seamanship manoeuvre. Normally, because of its size and inability to make small accurate course alterations in company with other ships, the tanker steered a steady course and maintained the same speed. She turned out her crane-like gantry with hoses attached so that they were dangling well outboard of the ship's side. When a steady course and speed had been achieved a signal was given and the warship to be refuelled steamed up alongside the tanker – just about a hundred feet away steering exactly the same course – and prepared to take the fuel from the tanker's hoses, which were turned out over a frequently confused and rough sea between the two vessels. A thin line was fired by rifle from the tanker to the receiving ship and, once recovered, hauled inboard. Attached to the thin gun line was a much thicker rope, which in turn when hauled inboard had the huge fuelling hose attached.

As the bridge crew concentrated on steaming close alongside the tanker, those on deck were focussed on heaving the huge hoses inboard and connecting them up to the appropriate fuelling point connection on the upper deck. It could be likened to a visit to your local garage to top up your tank, but the fuel hose is ten times bigger and locked into the fuelling position. When all was ready in both ships the order to 'Start pumping' was given and soon hundreds of tons of vital fuel, or in cleaner hoses, water, were pumped over from the tanker to the receiving ship.

It was an exercise in which the RFA seamen were well versed; after all, it was their entire raison d'etre. Their tankers were equipped, if necessary, to provide fuel and water to three ships at one time – one steaming close by on each side, with another astern taking its fuel from a hose streamed over the tanker's stern and retrieved inboard in the receiving ship. The latter was always the safest method of fuelling in very rough weather.

My job was simply to observe this exercise and to keep out of the way of men, hoses, fuel and flying gun lines. Witnessing my first RAS was a memorable occasion as I watched the frigate LOWESTOFT appear out of a beautiful sunrise, glide alongside, connect up her hoses, take onboard a few hundred tons of fuel and then disappear over the horizon. Simultaneously the tantalising smell of an early morning bacon sandwich wafted up from the galley far below (at which point I noted my stomach also needed a replenishment at sea and went below to seek the necessary).

After witnessing the fuel supply to LOWESTOFT and replenishing myself I checked my schedule to find I was to understudy the Captain for the rest of the day. At least he, I assumed, wouldn't have me cleaning out some obscure compartment in a set of appalling overalls.

I cautiously knocked at his cabin door at the appointed hour. He was a welcoming old sea dog who had doubtless spent most of his life at sea, and I noted by his accent he came from the other side of the Irish Sea.

After a chat with him over about my fifth cup of tea that day he quizzed me about what I had witnessed that morning. Had I been playing attention? He then started to outline his role as Captain of this twenty-year-old steam propelled vessel that had entered service just as World War II was ending. She had been in service supporting the fleet worldwide ever since.

In his broad Irish accent he went on to explain that apart from the obvious role of being responsible for the safe navigation and operation of his ship he also had a myriad of other jobs for which he took ultimate responsibility onboard. I was fascinated to see that he was also the closest thing the ship had to the manager of an off licence; he was responsible for the ordering, safe custody and sale of all the ship's beers, wines and spirits. I guess these transactions had gone wrong in the past (where there is booze and money my later experiences told me a "Racket" was potentially never far away) so the authorities ashore had insisted the Captain take both the ultimate and personal day-to-day responsibility. He was doubtless able to make the odd pound or two from this role buying at one price and selling onboard at another.

After a quick visit to the bridge to check the ship's position on that beautiful blue Mediterranean morning, and to note that she was indeed heading in the right direction for her next assignment, he told me it was time to return to his cabin for his next job of the day. No problem for me, I just followed behind... at least he hadn't mentioned grotty blue overalls.

Installed once again in his fine cabin he explained he was also the ship's Doctor. He doubtless saw my eyebrow lift a little so went on to explain that by British Merchant shipping regulations only a ship carrying over ninety-nine crewmembers or passengers needed a full time doctor onboard. As we had well under the required number, the Captain-cum-off licence manager stepped in to be the 'doc' too.

He explained that he had done a couple of DAYS training and was thus well equipped to carry out most medical needs or emergencies. As you can imagine, my eyebrows went a little higher.

He showed me two huge suitcases containing a wide variety of bottles, pillboxes, ointment tubes and an extensive variety of general medical kit. The suitcases had compartment after compartment packed with everything a 'Doctor' could possibly need. Mind you, some items looked as if they hadn't been out of the suitcase in the twenty years since the ship was built. I noted that not one of the pots and tubs was marked in any way, except with a number.

He then went on to show me his 'Doctor's Bible', a huge tome in which every conceivable medical condition – complete with symptoms – was listed in alphabetical order. A step-by-step guide was provided to enable the doctor to make an accurate diagnosis and supply the best cure for his patient. I noted some particularly graphic diagrams to help him along in his treatment of some ills – particularly sexually transmitted diseases.

None of this gave me any desire to encounter this Irishman in his professional capacity as the ship's doctor, and I made a mental note to wait until I was ashore in Malta before I went sick; there I would find plenty of highly qualified doctors and scores of pretty nurses.

Finally he informed me that as I was so seemingly interested he would let me sit in on one of his surgeries later than morning. I couldn't wait!

We took a stroll on the upper deck for a breath of fresh air and then on returning to his cabin I noticed half a dozen Maltese crewmen queuing up outside the cabin-cum-temporary surgery. Brave men these Maltese, I mused. (I later learned that a number of them, somewhat work shy, were regulars in the 'waiting room', as the passageway outside the Captain's cabin was known.)

His table covered with a baize tablecloth the Doctor Captain sat behind his manuals with his suitcases nearby, opened up and ready for action. I sat discreetly a short distance away from him as he interviewed his first patient in great depth. He inquired diligently of the patient's well-being and, it seemed to me, how every part of his body from head to toe was feeling that particular morning. He certainly gave him far more of his time than an average High Street GP would be able to give half a dozen patients in his waiting room. No wonder an appointment with 'the Doc' was a good wheeze to get time off work.

A lot of effort seemed to be going into this particular patient; he looked the picture of health to me but our Captain was taking no chances. I have little doubt in my own mind the guy was just up for a few hours off work and whatever diagnosis the Captain came up with would be fine by him.

Flicking backwards and forward in his Ship's Captain's Medical Guide it appeared he had two possible diagnoses in mind. Would it be the one on page 14 or the one on page 37? He was concentrating hard. Mmm... decisions... decisions...

At last he was close to making up his mind. Mustering all the skills of a Merchant Navy Captain with a two-day medical course behind him he was ready to make his reasoned judgement. The lad sat down... and the Captain announced that he had diarrhoea...

But now for the big one... the cure!

As all the potions and lotions in the suitcases were numbered no one knew what drugs or medicine they contained. A pot could contain anything from a potent drug to a simple analgesic. The system was simple – find a diagnosis and then the medical guide would indicate the cure, directing the 'doctor' to a numbered bottle or package in the suitcases. No fancy medical terminology was required.

The cure for this current case was simple; the patient was told he should take two pills from bottle number twenty-three twice a day until the problem ceased. Heading for his suitcase our ace medical man found that bottle number twenty-three was empty! Irish logic swung into play and the answer from here on was very simple; give the man one pill from pot number eleven and another from pot number twelve. This he did, and the man happily swallowed them down.

To this day I often wonder whether I should have in fact interfered with the 'physician's' actions. However, as an eighteen-year-old visiting trainee I lacked the confidence to get involved. But all was not lost – I am happy to report that this particular seaman was still alive – and seemingly well – when I left the ship some days later back in Malta!

CHAPTER TEN

CHRISTMAS .... MALTESE STYLE

As the minesweepers returned to harbour for the festive season the families of the crews made all their preparations to organise a typical English Christmas in the Maltese sun – albeit a weak sun in a windy and rain swept sky. Just like anywhere else, the kids were excited, especially with their sailor dads at home.

After a year as a Midshipman promotion to Sub Lieutenant was in the wind for me, and it would start on the first day of the rapidly approaching New Year. A week before Christmas an envelope arrived enclosing a Navy cheque for the vast sum of £65. This was a lot of money considering that all it was intended for was the purpose of commissioning a naval tailor to convert my Midshipman's uniform. A simple operation was required to remove the white tab on the jacket collar and add the symbolic gold stripe of a Sub Lieutenant around the cuff.

The cheque was too good to be spent on such sartorial nuances, especially as jackets were never worn onboard, and even more especially as I had spotted a black Ford Popular offered for sale in the local naval memorandum circulated around ships and shore establishments. It was on offer at exactly £65. Surely it already had my name on it…

Phoning the number given in the advert I found myself talking to the senior engineering officer of one of the larger warships in harbour. He had purchased the Ford as a 'run around' during his ship's brief visits to Malta. He was honest enough on the phone to say that its body wasn't the best but being the ship's senior engineer he could assure me the engine had been through his ships workshops - 'and the car goes like a horse.' I just had to see it.

I found the black Ford parked on the jetty near his ship. It was one of the old 'sit up and beg' types and it seemed a good deal to me even though the door on the driver's side was completely missing. However, someone had fitted an ingenious length of chain (of the type you see hanging from a conventional WC system) across the gap. Fortunately there were no MOT requirements on the Mediterranean island. Doors or no doors... did it really matter, especially in that climate?

My uniform cheque was soon exchanged for the Ford and within minutes I was the proud owner of my first car. There was one other 'slight problem' that the previous owner mentioned – the car had no starter motor - but, as he explained, by slipping it into gear while someone else pushed, it soon roared into life. The sales talk was correct – it never did fail to start (except once – more about that later).

As a new car owner and complete with a Maltese driving licence (I had learnt to drive in my father's car at home) I was suddenly very popular with the other junior officers of the squadron and was assured the local Wrens would now view me in a totally different light. Time would tell... second class driving certainly had to be better than first class walking, I told my many eager passengers endlessly.

One of its first outings was to take my fellow Midshipmen to Valletta one Saturday morning from our Msida base. On our return from the city centre we took a short cut back past the Police Headquarters and down a steep hill towards our base. Gently easing the car round a 90 degree bend onto the top of the hill the view of the creek opened up before me – as did the rear wheel attached to its half shaft, slowly overtaking us. As I gave orders for all the passengers (there always seemed to be four or even five of them) to put their weight over to the port side of the car I struggled to gain control of it and keep it upright with the sea below us fast approaching. I seemed to be winning... but the starboard wheel and half shaft beat me. Weaving a drunken path down the hill they ended up in the sea much to the amusement of passing pedestrians. As we brought the car to a rest – still perfectly upright - we all breathed a sigh of relief. We could all have been swimming, or worse.

I had plenty of help from the locals who had enjoyed the show to recover the wheel and shaft and then headed off to get some help to rebuild the car. It was no problem for one of the host of Maltese motor engineers who kept some very marginal vehicles on their roads, most well past their sell-by dates. They were more than willing to oblige. The car was back on the road within a few days, which was great because Christmas was just round the corner.

For all the Midshipmen (single men all of them) the festive season was greeted with a certain amount of apprehension. The ships were almost lifeless as the married men all headed to their temporary Maltese homes and their wives and families. As our virtually empty ships lay at their moorings Christmas seemed a bleak prospect. However, totally unbeknown to us, our Admiral – a real Admiral whom we never got to meet in our everyday life in the ships – had our best interests in mind. A fine invitation card complete with embossed crest and gold lettering arrived on the ships just a few days before Christmas inviting all of us Midshipmen to Christmas Day lunch with him and his lady wife.

As Midshipmen we were generally treated as a very low form of human life, accepted by our Sub Lieutenants, tolerated by the Lieutenants, but recognition of our existence by anyone of a higher rank was rare. To get a card indicating that 'Admiral Sir John and Lady Hamilton request the pleasure of your company to Christmas lunch' was something else… definitely a card to keep for the grandchildren's scrapbook. Mum back at home would be proud; we just all hoped his Christmas pudding would be as good as could be expected back at home.

Christmas Day dawned with a certain amount of nostalgia among us as we thought about our families and the festivities being enjoyed at home. Thank goodness we had Christmas lunch at the Admirals to look forward to…

Well before the appointed hour the five of us assembled on the jetty immaculately attired in our best uniforms as travel arrangements were discussed. It was universally agreed that a pound or two could be saved in taxi fares by taking my 'new' Ford to the Admiral's residence not a million miles from our berths alongside our new base near Fort St Angelo. Unaware of the exact location of the residence at Villa Portelli I was happy to follow instructions from my companions crammed into the car. A quick push down the jetty brought the engine to life, the passengers jumped in and we were away, the aroma of roast turkey and Christmas pudding in our minds if not yet in our nostrils.

Paying minimal attention to the instructions ushering forth from the back seat I had intended to park in the narrow streets close to the residence and walk the last few yards. My Ford was fine for a Midshipman's trip to the beach but not exactly 'de rigeur' for an official visit to the Admiral's residence. My navigator had other ideas....Before I knew it however we were passing through the huge oak gates of the residence, which had been opened for our arrival. My "friend" considered this some kind of joke! Negotiating the last few yards to the beautiful residence through immaculately manicured gardens, I had no alternative but to draw up right in front of the house to disgorge my passengers. We were welcomed by no less than a Royal Marine in full traditional dress uniform, complete with white gloves, positioned at the stone portico. He was so placed to open our car door (if it had existed) and indicated where we should park and find our way to meet the great man and his wife.

This was not quite what I had planned. My passengers were quick to alight leaving me looking straight in the steely eyes of the Royal Marine saluting whilst he at the same time was looking for a door to open for me. There was no door to open of course. I'm not sure who was the more embarrassed, but worse was yet to come. The Admiral and his wife appeared at the doorway. Genuinely amused to see the Ford before them, I had a sneaking feeling that most of their other visitors were obviously more used to arriving in much smarter means of transport – most complete with doors. All my compatriots had fast headed for the sherry on offer on a silver tray. I was left to park the car and then it happened – it cut out dead... dead... dead! The first and only time under my ownership!

Whilst the Admiral took his guests into the house his wife and the Royal Marine pushed the dead car, with me sat in it steering, into the stables some twenty yards away. To say I knew that feeling where one simply wants the earth to open up and be able to slip into whatever cavern appeared would be a major under-estimation of the situation that existed that Christmas morning.

Eventually regaining my composure and reassured by my smiling hostess that all was well I headed for the house and the tray of sherry glasses. I had earned it and sank the first in one quick gulp. I glimpsed a raised eyebrow from my hostess... but I was ready for six more.

We went on to spend a most enjoyable Christmas day with the Admiral and his wife. He was a most charming man for whom the real meaning of Christmas was apparent and he was more than willing to open his home and spend his day with us, his most junior officers. The day's festivities included playing very silly games with dustbin lids and corks on a string, I seem to remember. His gesture will never be forgotten – or our grand arrival at his fine residence overlooking Grand Harbour, either!

Word rapidly spread re the Midshipman's Christmas lunch and my car became well known, and a marked vehicle on the Maltese roads thereafter.

Time was rapidly approaching however for my return to the UK so the car had to be sold. It raised the required £65 from an Army Officer so I was back in pocket and able to get my uniform alterations completed before flying home for a new job.

CHAPTER ELEVEN

OFF TO ICELAND

I was sad to leave. Life in Malta had been great: warm climate, good job… it was as if the taxpayer had specifically provided me with personal travel facilities to tour the Med to see all the ports and harbours. I was enjoying life to the full and had certainly learnt a lot, mainly about my future career as a naval officer but also a considerable amount about women. Having grown up as an only child in an all boys' school - consequently I suspect being uncomfortable in the presence of women, my time in Malta had been a crash course in life or at least that part of it. However, some eighteen months after arriving in the island it was time for me to be moved on to let another young officer take my place.

After a short period of leave back at home in Gosport, where nothing seemed to have changed, even if I had, I found myself heading north to Rosyth dockyard in Scotland (the new posting had come through whilst I was still in Malta). The joke was that here I was in the Royal Navy, living in the Portsmouth area and some-one with a sense of humour decided to send me to Scotland. As I drove my new mini (with doors on both sides) towards my new posting I was trying hard to think of any similarities between the Malta job and the one I was heading for… and I could come up with no answers at all.

Two huge World War II Escort maintenance ships, GIRDLE NESS and

75

DUNCANSBY HEAD had been berthed together at Rosyth to provide accommodation mainly for ships' companies from ships in refit; it was to one of those I headed, to show off my rapidly disappearing Mediterranean suntan to anyone who expressed any interest. (They didn't!)

These huge ships were to be 'home' for a number of weeks. Their days as maintenance vessels were long past – they were 95% empty with only a scattering of cabins, mess decks, galleys and offices in use. Their function as accommodation ships was a swansong for them in the Navy before being hauled off to the scrapyard. Every footstep echoed as the few souls aboard, no more than a dozen of us, walked around the cavernous hulks. It wasn't quite like the good life in Malta in these huge cold empty steel boxes that had become my new home. There was a shortage of accommodation in this part of Scotland so we slept on one ship and ate on the other. It felt very strange living in these eerie and echoey hulks – especially after those fantastic days in Malta.

Days on the hulks were soon over – I was there to join my new ship in the dockyard working onboard by day but returning to the hulks by night to sleep in my new "home". It was not to last long we would soon be heading to Iceland. The suntan would doubtless disappear soon.

The tiny frigate BLACKWOOD was completing a refit and once again I was to be the most junior officer on board. The frigate was destined to be the leader of the Navy's largest squadron – the Fishery Protection Squadron comprising half a dozen frigates which patrolled to distant waters, a dozen Ton class coastal minesweepers that patrolled the UK coastal waters and even a couple of tiny Ham class minesweepers capable of entering the shallowest waters. A ship of BLACKWOOD'S size would normally be commanded by a Lieutenant Commander, but we were to be a 'top heavy' command as the senior ship of the squadron. Our Captain wore the full four stripes of a Captain RN and everyone else in the wardroom seemed to be a Squadron officer who, I was soon to learn, when some dismal sea time was planned off Norway or Iceland, tried to make instant plans to visit one of their ships in a more acceptable part of the world.

Once again I had won the ship's Correspondence Officer job, probably because I was the most junior officer and it's the job no one wants to do. It was pretty much the same job as in a minesweeper but this time more sailors were 'on the books' and I had Petty Officer (Writer) Hooper to take the strain. The Wrens of Rosyth were safe – I wouldn't be chasing them for their typing skills. I was also onboard as an (as yet) unqualified Officer of the Watch destined to spend up to eight hours of my day on the bridge, responsible for the ship's safety and navigation. It was obvious to me at an early stage that the other bridge watch keepers had one aim and objective in life – namely to 'get Critchley qualified'. Who could blame them? It was a nuisance for them having to supervise me.

I was particularly pleased to see my parade-training officer from Dartmouth days as another new arrival in the wardroom; Bill Smith was to prove himself to be a great messmate. We had a good understanding; he being a World War II seaman found all the modern technology on the bridge and Operations room a bit beyond his comprehension, so I did his watches when we were 'playing proper warships' exercising – and he did mine when seasickness once again got the better of me! (Not surprisingly, the seas off Iceland were to prove to be far worse than the Med.) As the last weeks of the refit passed we deserted our accommodation in 'the hulks' and prepared our new ship – and eventually commissioned her with due ceremony under the command of Captain Ian Campbell RN. A fishin' we were to go!

We had to spend time 'working up' to make sure we were indeed up and running properly with a totally new crew and ready to take our position as Leader of the Squadron. Setting sail from Rosyth we embarked on our first taste of sea time onboard, which comprised an anti clockwise circuit of the UK to get our act together and get used to working onboard as a team. We were to 'enjoy' the delights of the Pentland Firth for the first time as we set out round Scotland. Our tiny 1000ton frigate bounced around mercilessly as we battled our way through those infamous waters between Scotland and the Orkneys. Memories of that first earlier Patras trip in my minesweeper flooded back – as did the many trips to the ship's side…

Our first port of call was Milford Haven in 'little England beyond Wales', a most beautiful part of the country. Securing to the jetty at the Navy's mining depot we were in town to fly the flag for the Royal Navy at the local celebrations of some local historic event. It was an interesting visit for a young Sub Lieutenant; after the inevitable first night in harbour cocktail party onboard we were all whisked off to a local dance. It was very obvious that most of the ship's officers were way out of their depth in the assembled company. Many were old enough to be the dancers' fathers – but they bravely attended – all in the course of duty. As the 'baby' of the wardroom and, of course, with my dancing lessons of Dartmouth to draw on, it was obviously my job to take the lead. I stepped out attired in my best uniform to show the others how to do it. Approaching a smart young local lass who I spotted across the crowded room I offered her the opportunity to be whisked around the dance floor by a dashing young naval officer – the only one in fact the ship could produce. It came as a hard blow to my ego when she responded to my request with a quick, 'Sorry Granddad – ask me mate, I'm sweating meself already!' It was time to slink back to the ship… at the good old age of just twenty…

Slipping out of the haven on the morning tide we headed for Portland to be put through our paces for a few days (other ships spent many weeks at the place) by the local Admirals staff and then on to Portsmouth for a weekend off. It was good to be able to take my parents onboard one of Her Majesty's ships for the first (and it transpired last) time. They appreciated seeing my 'home from home' and Mother in particular wanted to see where I slept and where the food was cooked of course.

It was then back up the east coast to Rosyth to prepare for the first trip to Iceland. The Type 14 frigates, of which BLACKWOOD was one, were cheap and cheerful in concept and certainly not designed to be let loose in the far distant waters of the North Atlantic. Even after just a few weeks round the UK coast repairs were already necessary. It was a welcome time for a few weeks to relax and to take time to catch up on washing clothes, paying bills and all those other necessary chores.

With Criminal Intent…

It was whilst serving in BLACKWOOD I had my first brush with the law.

As the ship's Correspondence Officer it was one of my duties to pay the ship's company, in cash. Whilst the ship was alongside in Rosyth Naval base when in Scotland, for some strange reason her accounts and the men and women who kept them were at the Minesweepers base on the other side of the River Forth at Port Edgar – HMS LOCHINVAR. It was a fortnightly, or shortly before sailing, ritual to drive over the Forth Road bridge to Port Edgar at South Queensferry in my faithful Mini accompanied by a trusty Senior rating, always with a pick axe handle to repel all robbers, to collect what for me was an inconceivably large sum of money for over one hundred sailors' pay.

It was normally a quick and easy job, carried out just hours before the ship's company were due to be paid so that the amount of time the money sat in my tiny ship's safe was minimal.

On this particular day all went well until it was time to leave the sleepy confines of the South Queensferry base. Despite the base being on its last legs – having been built in World War I and by then earmarked for closure – it still warranted a Ministry of Defence Police presence on the main gate to guard a handful of minesweepers alongside and a few piles of minesweeping equipment. It must have been one of the Ministry of Defence Police force's most boring jobs, especially as it was needed round the clock.

As I approached the gate heading back to Rosyth in my Mini with the ship's company pay on the floor of the car in what resembled a rep's bag, the car was stopped by a young constable who looked young enough to be straight out of training. He was soon to be identified as one of those who had obviously done the John McEnroe Charm Course – and failed miserably.

There were no pleasantries whatsoever; no 'Please Sir' or 'Would you mind' - I was simply told to 'Geet oot.' On enquiring why, I was told that it was his right to stop me and search my car (he virtually quoted the paragraph from the training manual). Counting up to ten before speaking I politely told him that as I had a considerable sum of Her Majesty's money in the car with over one hundred sailors waiting at Rosyth to catch the necessary public transport home it would be much appreciated if my car was not the one he chose to search that morning. I was wasting my breath; it was like talking to a brick wall. His reply was simple: 'Geet oot.' I counted to ten again and then politely asked if I could speak to his Sergeant. The reply was more emphatic: 'Geet oot!'

I finally got the message. Leaving my Petty Officer with the cash I leapt past the constable and headed for the guardhouse where his colleague was taking his mid morning snack whilst completing the Daily Record crossword. I thought that this more mature officer would at least see the reason my neck and face were beginning to glow with rage. None of it. 14 down in the crossword was of far greater importance to MoD Plod No 2 than my predicament. Eventually he deigned to speak: 'If my colleague wants to search your car sir, he wants to search your car sir – and I suggest you are seen to give your full co-operation before I have to report this matter to my superiors.' Unless I was going to burst a blood vessel and be removed from the scene by ambulance I was obviously going to have to comply with 'the request'.

So I returned to the car. To add insult to injury it started to rain but that didn't stop MoD Plod No 1 demanding that I take everything out of the vehicle. Out came the screen wash, torch, AA road map, old sweet wrappers, Green Shield stamp book, gloves… but that wasn't good enough to satisfy him. Round to the back of the car we went and out came the jack, suitcase (contents various), spare wheel, rug, and spare petrol container. Surely he would be happy now?

'Just take the back seat oot of the car now - sir.' He had great difficulty speaking the last word through clenched teeth but he managed it - just.

79

Where would all this end? Would he expect me to dismantle the engine next? Out came the entire back seat and that really made his day – a smile started to spread across his cold unfriendly face. His eyes actually lit up! He had seen the contraband he was after. Underneath where the back seat had been fixed lay one two-inch paintbrush, complete with the traditional broad arrow on it indicating it was indeed HM Government property. He was now a very happy man!

Having made his find I could almost hear the handcuffs jangling in his pockets… and were his lips trying to rehearse the correct wording for him to arrest me? No – he simply indicated that I could replace what now resembled the contents of a jumble sale spread round the car and report to him in his office. By this time I was beginning to see the funny side of this charade. We had already missed the time for the ship's company to be paid so I thought I had just as well to play along with Super Cop.

Stood solemnly in front of his ancient and very rickety desk I was invited to make a statement as to how the item of HM Naval stores came to be 'smuggled' out of HMS LOCHINVAR and 'secreted' under the seat of my car registration number EBK284C I rolled up my sleeves slightly so they wouldn't be marked by the ink as I assumed fingerprinting was next on the agenda for paint brush thieves (it wasn't). I had no idea whatsoever how a brush (paint for the use of, in correct navy jargon) ended up under the seat of the car, and said so in my statement – but that really wasn't good enough for Super Cop. And no, I couldn't ring the ship and tell them what was going on – I had to keep filling in his wretched form…

Eventually we were released from the clutches of the gendarmerie and allowed to proceed, 'Pending further enquiries and action'. Had I stolen the entire bagful of money in the car I would have felt somewhat guilty but as a first offence paint-brush thief I began to smile as I drove back across the road bridge; the event had been too silly for words.

Back at base the ship's company were of course all waiting eagerly to go on Christmas leave and wondering what was causing the hold up; by the time I appeared I was more than an hour late. Erring on the side of caution I told my Captain what had happened and, upset as he was that many of his ship's company travel plans had been disrupted, he too thought the paintbrush incident had been a huge, almost unbelievable, joke.

I was due to travel south to Hampshire but thanks to the 'Lochinvar incident' I too had missed my train. It was time to make alternative plans to get home for Christmas; the next best arrangement would be to catch the night train from Edinburgh to Kings Cross. As I packed my bags I reasoned that I'd heard the last

TENBY – seen here in Grand Harbour Malta whilst on one of her routine three month Cadet training cruises from the UK. Malta was always a popular port of call and the welcome cordial.
(*Syd Goodman Collection*)

The Minesweeper STUBBINGTON in calmer seas leaves Lazaretto Creek Malta for another minesweeping exercise. The six minesweepers in the Seventh Minesweeping Squadron roamed the entire length of the Mediterranean exercising with other NATO vessels and much enjoying port visits before or after any exercises.

(*TCA Collection*)

A sister ship of the Greek Naval ship SALAMINIA shortly after World War II. These vessels were built in the USA in 1943, immediately transferred to the Royal Navy, and then taken over by the Greek Navy in 1946. They served until the mid 1960's.

(*Author's Collection*)

There was a huge requirement for officers to specialise in the submarine service in the early sixties...the new Polaris submarines were being built and would need large numbers of officers when completed. A few days in THERMOPYLAE operating on and below the surface soon convinced me I was not to be one of them!

(Portsmouth Royal Naval Museum)

Spic and span.....HMS BLACKWOOD seen on her delivery from the shipbuilders. These tiny Type 14 frigates were a cheap and very basic vessel designed to counter the post war Soviet submarine threat. Their peacetime role included the need to police the UK fishery limits and support our fishing vessels but they often did not perform well in the mountainous seas often encountered around Iceland.

(Syd Goodman Collection)

With her decks packed with Scimitar, Sea Vixen and Gannet aircraft ARK ROYAL looks a fine sight here at anchor in the Far East. She conducted the very first Beira patrol in the Mozambique channel – but not without loss of life. (*Ken Kelly Colection*)

HMS EASTBOURNE – a sister ship of TENBY. These ships were the forerunners of the very successful Leander class – their hulls being practically the same. Four ships of the class were used to train young officers from the Britannia Royal Naval college at Dartmouth – for most, their first taste of life at sea in the Royal Navy.

(Author's Collection)

Slowly sailing home from the Mediterranean and much needing time in the dockyard
to repair a number of defects that effected her speed. All the oars onboard (normally
used in her ships boats) were – apparently - pressed into service as she steamed past-
the other ships of the squadron before entering port.   (*Author's Collection*)

With the huge supertanker TORREY CANYON aground on the Sevenstones reef off
Lands End (March 1967) every small vessel – including the former minesweeper
ODIHAM seen here - that the Navy could identify were pressed into service. Fitted
with some basic spraying equipment and hundreds of gallons of detergent they all
sailed from Falmouth each day to try and save Cornish and French beaches from an
ecological disaster – the first around our shores. There were no plans to follow – it
was a first!   (*TCA Collection*)

The sad sight of the M/V LENNART after her rescue off a lee shore on the Isle of Wight earlier that day. She had sailed against all advice from Sweden and was lost and broken down just a mile from the shore when rescued by EASTBOURNE. Her crew – heading for the "good life" in the West Indies - had a very lucky escape.
(*Author's Collection*)

LOFOTEN. This old War War II veteran Landing Ship (Tank) was converted into "Britain's latest aircraft carrier" in 1964 and was used extensively to train the crews of the Royal Navy's new Wessex Mk 3 helicopters in deep waters off the south west of England – far away from their base and vital fuel supplies.

(Syd Goodman Collection)

of the paintbrush incident: somewhere in the head office of the Scottish MoD Plodery a wise old sergeant would read Super Cop's report, have him in the office, offer him a few words of wisdom and deposit the statements in the wastepaper basket. Then, without a further thought about it, I gathered my bags together and headed for the ship's freezer to claim a parcel of frozen cod, which was to accompany me on my journey home.

Perhaps I should just explain why I was about to set off south accompanied by a VERY large cod. It was the custom of the trawler men that when we went to their vessels to give emergency aid or some unplanned maintenance we were permitted to take some sort of 'a bag' with us to collect a quantity of fish as payment. Initially we would take a small holdall but the more trips we made over the weeks the bigger the bags became, until eventually the fishermen, uncomplaining it must be said, were stuffing our 'catch' into huge Post Office parcel sacks. The cod was always succulent and far larger than you'll ever see in any fishmongers, and so fresh that many were still alive and kicking when taken to the ships galley onboard!

Struggling back in a tiny dinghy with a huge quantity of fish was never easy, and attempting to negotiate the ship's side with a very heavy canvas sack while the frigate wallowed in the seaway was nothing less than pure comedy... or maybe that should be black comedy as now I can see that it was often verging on the downright dangerous.

Once onboard the rules were simple after the chef had taken his portion of the catch; anyone who wanted a fish (one per person) would tie a parcel tag through its tail with the claimant's name on it, and it was then stored in the ship's freezer until our return to port. The remainder of 'the haul' was eaten, and what a fine gourmet experience that was, better than any of your fancy fish restaurants advertised in the best guide books.

When we were about to go on leave, the ship's fridges were open for anyone to 'claim their cod'. A few sheets of newspaper were wrapped around the fine specimen of the sea and off went Mr Cod on leave with his owner. For most, the short trip to the Rosyth married quarters soon saw the beast in Mrs Sailor's deep freeze, but for those who lived further afield it was trickier. The fish – just lightly wrapped in newspaper, remember – left the naval base and travelled wherever the owner was heading. Rail passengers were in for a surprise as the heat of any train had an amazing effect on the once frozen block of fish!

With my naval officer's uniform left behind in my tiny wardrobe I was off with a colleague from another ship to find my way south on the night train. Now in those days junior naval officers were genuinely not well paid so we were definitely not prepared to buy British Rail sleeper tickets on the night train south. We had our own system…

At the back of Edinburgh Waverley station was a small corner shop where we always bought our 'tickets' for a good night's sleep on the train. Shortly before they closed for the night we would nip in and purchase a couple of cans of Crosse and Blackwell diced mixed vegetable soup (medium size). We had a well-practised routine: once on board the train, whilst others made themselves comfortable for the night in their sleeper cabins, we found ourselves a standard compartment of the type in service in those days where two comfortable bench seats opposite each other had a sliding door to keep the compartment private from the passageway outside. These compartments were always in short supply and sitting up all night with four or five other passengers was no joke, but if one could make an early claim to a compartment, lie out full length and keep other travellers out a perfectly acceptable night could be enjoyed as the train wound its way south to London.

It was at this point the tins of Crosse and Blackwell came in handy. Once a compartment had been 'claimed' the tins were opened and their contents spread carefully in the passageway outside and slightly into the compartment. It always guaranteed that no further travellers attempted to join us (I suspect it was the diced carrots that sent people away). It didn't however prevent the Guard making us clear up the mess early next morning, normally as the train passed through Watford, but by then the soup had solidified on to the lino of the passageway thanks to the heating pipes below so it proved easy to remove. No harm done and a great nights sleep!

By morning the smell of the 'frozen' cod, which had spent the night on the luggage rack of the well-heated compartment, was another issue. I soldiered on with it, carrying it across platforms as I changed on and off the underground trains to continue my journey to Portsmouth. Eventually I had to give in and somewhere between Havant and Portsmouth I had to jettison my package onto the track – the other passengers were becoming hostile. So near to mother's freezer too, but it had to go for the cats of Fratton to enjoy no doubt later that evening when the trains stopped for the day.

Soon I was back with my parents at Alverstoke preparing for the hectic schedule of my 'other life' as a Christmas postman. Having served my apprenticeship on a previous assignment as a mere foot soldier flogging round the letter boxes of the town I had been promoted to the parcel department for this particular Christmas period. An 0600 start saw our parcels loaded into a hired furniture van and then all the other posties and myself were off to Forton Road for a very acceptable breakfast at the local greasy spoon café before moving on to Rowner to start our parcel distribution for the day.

The only problem was that days before I left Scotland a memo from local naval headquarters had been circulating in the wardrooms of Her Majesty's ships saying that it had come to the Admiral's attention that Naval Officers were moonlighting 'out of hours' and the big man considered that taxi driving, bar work and a bit of part time driving instructing were not appropriate work for his officers to undertake. This was to 'stop forthwith'. I muttered agreement with the Admiral's sentiment as I passed the memo on to a fellow officer but neglected to mention I had been accepted, and was expected to sign on, again for a second Christmas as a temporary parcel postman. At least there were 300 miles between the ship and the main sorting office at South St Gosport, so the chances of being found out were minimal!

A couple of hours into my first round found me in a huge furniture van on what was obviously a naval married quarters estate. After I'd banged for some time on one of the glazed front doors a bleary-eyed male gathered some clothing round him ready to face the chilly morning air as he opened his door. I don't know who had the greatest surprise – the 'moonlighting' postman or the Petty Officer from HMS BLACKWOOD way north in Rosyth. He sputtered something like a 'Good morning sir – didn't expect to see you here this morning,' as I muttered something about him and his family having a Happy Christmas – and scurried, red faced, back to the safety of my furniture van.

Not a word was ever said when we both returned to the ship in Rosyth two weeks later. Bless him! But moonlighting was the least of my problems. There was plenty of other trouble brewing just around the corner…

On arrival back onboard after Christmas I was summoned to my Captain's cabin to be told that my 'criminal report' had arrived. It was time to face the music regarding The Case Of The Stolen Paintbrush. I couldn't believe it - the police did in fact mean business. Despite having much better things to do with his time as the Commanding Officer of a Squadron of Royal Naval warships he had made a suitable appointment with the local Admiral, donned his best suit and, complete with sword and medals, headed off to the Pitraevie HQ to complain on my behalf. To no avail. Both he – and I – lost! Neither senior officer could alter the situation; I had simply been caught with a paintbrush that wasn't mine. It was Government property; therefore I was to be 'logged' (mention of the offence was to be placed on my personal records). My criminal record had started! Hey ho!

Thank goodness it was time to escape Scotland and get back to sea. We were to flog up to Iceland to patrol the fishing grounds, generally keeping an eye on things and giving any assistance required by British fishing vessels in the area. Although there was no 'Cod War' as such underway at the time, events were obviously building up for the next one.

It was clear from an early stage that the Hull and Grimsby trawlers that operated in those hostile waters went to sea to carry out their maintenance, rather than complete it in harbour in a more normal manner. As soon as one of Her Majesty's vessels was spotted by the trawlers on the horizon it wouldn't be long before the radio would crackle into life and a gruff trawler skipper enquire 'Navy ship... Navy ship... do yer have any radar mechanics onboard?' Or something similar. We would frequently oblige and sail close enough to the trawler to enable the required technician to cross the seas in a small rubber dinghy to scramble onboard the trawler with his bag of tools to see if he could indeed oblige. My captain 'volunteered' me to accompany our technical whiz kid on one occasion when his radar skills were required.

Tackling the boiling seas between the two vessels in a rubber dinghy was something I wouldn't want to have to do too often. As the mechanic and I scrambled onboard the trawler, men shrouded in yellow oilskins having interrupted their endless gutting of fish were keen to help. Soon they were back to their duties, hardly lifting their eyes from their flashing knives as we gained our bearings and headed for the bridge to assess the problem. A warm greeting from the young skipper who looked as if he had neither slept nor shaved for days showed he was obviously grateful that we had brought one of Her Majesty's vessels to his aid. Once the technical guru had started to take the back of the radar off (having brushed aside many years' accumulation of dust) the skipper offered us a drink... 'I was about to have one meself.' Feeling none too bright in the prevailing sea conditions even the thought of a cup of coffee had me declining the offer rapidly. He obviously didn't hear me as he soon reappeared on the bridge clutching an Old Spice shaving mug full to the very top with whisky and thrust it into my hand. Not my ideal refreshment at any time and just before eight on a blustery autumn morning with a gale on the way it was far from welcome... I hate to admit it to any Scotsman who happens to be reading this but the mug went back on the chart table, not a drop of the liquid went down my throat and as quickly and discreetly as I could I'm sorry to say that I poured the 'wee dram' over the ships side.

---

* Readers who remember these times well may be interested in our book *The Royal Navy and the Cod Wars* (Captain Andrew Welch RN) published by Maritime Books. A fascinating text illustrated by a collection of amazing photographs.

Fishery Protection duties on this trip were to be a Monday to Friday job around the agreed fishing limit. The occasional Icelandic patrol boats would appear and, apart from the odd shaking of fists as they passed, relations were reasonably cordial. By Friday night we were in Reykjavik harbour entertaining Icelandic coastguards and fishermen with Scottish Duty Free drinks – seemingly all the best of friends. It was a funny old world. How things would change a few years later as the next Cod War started.

It was during these long Icelandic patrols that I was eventually tested by Ken Snow, the Squadron navigator, to see if I was indeed suitable to be given my Bridge Watchkeeping certificate; that final, important, piece of paper to indicate that, after all the training, the great day had arrived (give or take a few hiccups) and I was now considered safe and competent to carry out a bridge watch – by day or night. The certificate was soon in my hands much to the delight of my messmates who wasted no time in putting me to good use! That very first night I was on the bridge shortly before 0400 to carry out the morning watch. On my own – in charge - for the first time onboard something approaching a proper warship - it was a good feeling. I had at last made it – Mum and Dad would be proud. So doubtless would Curly.

As we headed back to Rosyth from our fish patrol, a signal was sent to the Ministry of Defence indicating that I had been awarded the all-important piece of paper, which meant that I was at last useful enough to be appointed to any ship as a trained seaman watchkeeping officer throughout the Fleet.

News travels fast… Even before the ship reached Rosyth a signal was back from the Ministry saying I was being reappointed to the mighty aircraft carrier ARK ROYAL – again as a watchkeeper. The plan to get me qualified as soon as possible had backfired on the BLACKWOOD officers: I was off! The thought of going to the largest ship in the fleet was good news indeed, anything but Icelandic fish patrols!

Although I knew the name of my new ship the biggest secret of the day was where she was in the world. She was believed to be somewhere in the Far East but that was pretty vague. However, on the international stage things were not good in Africa. Rhodesian Prime Minister Ian Smith had declared his Unilateral Declaration of Independence (UDI) and the country was heading for a major crisis. So, the rumour around the naval fraternity was that ARK ROYAL was to stand by for use however the UK government of the day decided best. There was a definite possibility that she and her aircraft would be called upon to help out in Southern Africa in some way. However, no one could give me any more accurate information. I was thus sent home on leave and told to gather all my white tropical uniforms together and 'await further instructions'.

CHAPTER TWELVE

TO AFRICA...

My wait did not last long. About a week later the call came that, I (along with around a hundred others) was to report to RAF Hendon in North London for 'onward movement' to the mighty Ark.

Anxious to know what exactly was afoot we were soon told we were to spend the night at Hendon and the next day buses were to take us across London to Gatwick airport for an RAF trooping flight to Nairobi; an odd place, miles from the sea, for sailors to join an aircraft carrier. We were told that our movement to East Africa was in itself 'classified' and we were not even to tell our families of our intended destination. The plot thickened...

Gatwick was an unusual departure point for an RAF flight as RAF Lyneham or Brize Norton were usually the normal places to report for overseas flights. On arrival we simply looked for an RAF check-in desk to get rid of all our luggage. There was none. A hundred sailors made a search as we fanned out through Gatwick to, hopefully, find a single representative of the RAF in the huge terminal. At last an RAF corporal was located reading his morning paper; he was nonplussed to discover dozens of sailors deposited on his patch and appeared to know nothing about us. So the whole thing was a big secret even to the RAF! He had no RAF flights on his clipboard for that day but wandered off to get some more details from his seniors somewhere at the end of a telephone line. Piles of baggage were made with a few men allocated to keep an eye on them whilst the rest of the mob wandered away to browse the cafes, shops and bars.

Eventually our RAF contact appeared explaining that the RAF would not be flying us to Nairobi; they had subcontracted the flight to Caledonian Airways. Our hopes were raised that something was at last happening as sailors appeared from all round the airport and descended on the Caledonian check in-desk.

So Caledonian were to fly us, but no one had told their check-in girls. More phone calls were made, as the whole saga was beginning to wear thin. The result of the calls? We were told that yes, Caledonian did have the contract, but the plane was unserviceable and in any case it was at that moment in Frankfurt! As a hundred sailors muttered with a varying degree of volume we all went in search of the corporal who had disappeared into the depths of the terminal. When we eventually found him, his only option was to summon the buses back from North London to take us back to RAF Hendon. It was gone 8pm when some very angry sailors and a clutch of officers went in search of their midday meal – and supper too. The sailors even thought they would get their daily tot of rum. Some hope at an RAF base!

Another early start was necessary the next day to cross London by our buses in the rush hour for our flight to Africa. Descending on the Caledonian desk amongst all the holidaymakers we were met by a new shift of check-in girls who, again, had no knowledge of our plight from the previous day. They checked their paperwork… and checked it again. As fingers were drummed on the counter more calls were made… it turned out our plane was still on the ground in Germany, with no estimate of a departure time!

As the day ticked by Caledonian eventually admitted defeat; they gave us plenty of coffee but no hope of an aircraft. It became the turn of another airline to have the delight of the movement of one hundred matelots to their check in desk; this time it was Dan Air who, we were told, now had the contract to fly us, but – guess what - no one had told Dan Air! More chaos as voices were raised louder and louder in protest. Dan Air indeed had a contract – with the ink on it hardly dry - but no aircraft. Our patience was running out…

There was nothing else to do but whistle up the buses and head back for RAF Hendon. This was becoming a very familiar trip…

By now the few senior officers in our group were beginning to play the rank card and demand some answers. As we went to bed that night we were assured our early shake the next morning was necessary and we would be flying that day, but we were not confident. We were fast becoming Gatwick commuters...

And on the third day... the group of happy travellers was seen wearily arriving at Gatwick by now complete with copious packs of playing cards, newspaper and magazines to pass yet another day in what was rapidly becoming our second home.

Met by a real RAF officer in uniform, this time oozing apologies, we brushed passed him muttering that the RAF would not be moving their own people like this. We headed for, once again, the Caledonian desk where yes, they were expecting us again – Dan Air having given up their contract with no aircraft to use.

Was it really possible we were going to get airborne at last? A gleaming Britannia aircraft awaited us on the tarmac this time. We walked out to the aircraft in snake like fashion and ascended the steps as fast as we could to get some shelter from the wind and rain of a typical spring Gatwick day. As we were ushered onboard our RAF friend gave us all a railway voucher for a ticket from Nairobi to Mombasa. The 'secret' plot to get us to ARK ROYAL was now taking shape...

On entering the cabin of the plane we were met by a sight normally reserved for aircraft engineers boarding a plane in the midst of a major overhaul. All the internal panelling had been removed revealing a mass of wires, pulleys and hydraulic pipes threading their way the length of the aircraft and around the egg-shaped windows. On inquiring from the airline staff why our aircraft had a 'half built' look about it we were told that the plane was being pressed into military service from its normal duties of transporting tourists around the world. Carpets, panelling and any extras had all been removed to reduce the total weight, and stacked up and strapped into the rear of the plane were empty 40-gallon oil drums.

Were we going to make the Gatwick/East Africa trip in one hop and at some stage perhaps these drums would provide the extra fuel needed for our epic journey? The truth was that in the fast deteriorating situation in Rhodesia there was a real chance that fuel to keep the landlocked nation of Zambia provided with vital oil would have to be flown in, in a handful of 40 gallon oil drums.... and then only just a few drums at a time. Not quite the same as the flow of oil sent to Rhodesia down the pipeline from Beira in happier times.

In our seats and ready to get underway (some three days late) all we wanted to do was to get airborne but after the normal safety brief we had to endure the sales pitch from the airline staff. Every time a stewardess picked up her intercom microphone an automatic recording of the dreaded goatskin piano (bagpipes) would herald the statement 'Caledonian Airways, Scotland's only independent airline, would like to announce that...' There were no exceptions; whatever the announcement, be it that the drinks trolley was about to be trundled through the cabin or that seat belts should be secured, we had to endure the same recording. It soon became more than a little irritating!

At last we were airborne through the mists of Gatwick as the whispering giant – as the faithful Britannia was always know – climbed to its cruising height. But 'whispering' giant this aircraft definitely was not! Not only was the whispering frequently interrupted by the goatskin piano announcements but, it transpired, the rear door to the plane had either not been secured properly or was twisted; a really loud howling was emanating from the door and its frame. Even before we were at cruising height it was obvious this flight wasn't going to be smooth. As we headed across the English Channel it wasn't clear what was worse, the screaming rear door or the interminable bagpipe-accompanied announcements. The Captain eventually apologised for the 'slightly excessive noise' (he was up front – he should wander back towards our seats, we all thought) but added that we would be arriving in Rome in a few hours time and the problem would be solved there.

We sat back praying the staff would have no announcements to make and idly passed away the hours. As we made our way south in this semi stripped aircraft, watching the wires and pulleys move as the pilot or autopilot adjusted the flaps and rudder kept us amused.

The last announcement before landing was that the staff would be handing out vouchers for a snack on the ground at Rome. Brainwashed by bagpipes we assumed it would be haggis of course...

It was a great feeling as we roared down the runway at Rome's Fiumicino airport... the reverse thrust roared into action and eventually we came to a halt at our allocated apron. Only once more did we have to listen to the bagpipes and the latest from 'Scotland's only independent airline...' as we were told that repairs would be carried out to the door and that it was hoped we would enjoy our snack on the ground etc etc. There was a dash for the doors...

A posse of matelots headed for the refreshment bar at an ever quickening pace, every single one clutching a blue card that we were assured would provide us suitable sustenance for the next leg of our journey. Had we arrived at Rome's other airport, at Ciampino, our vouchers would have been valid – but not at this one! We had either landed at the wrong airport or simply been given the wrong vouchers. A hundred hungry matelots without a single Lira between them were thus soon encamped, unfed, in the departure lounge with a good view of our whispering giant taking on fuel whilst a small army of technical staff ambled on and off the plane. There obviously was no hurry.

Within a couple of hours a mercifully 'bagpipe free' announcement indicated it was time to re-board our plane. We were ready to head south as the Italian sun slipped below the horizon and our plane taxied to the runway and then aimed for the skies above.

It was soon obvious that the 'technical experts' provided on the ground at Rome had carried out a fine in depth engineering appraisal of the situation. Bringing all their expertise to bear they had come up with a hi-tech solution; they had stuffed toilet paper round the edge of the closed door. Whilst some of us were trying to decide whether to attack the intercom system with any weapon to hand or hijack the plane back to Rome others sat back to watch the wires and pulleys again – but as they did so, wonder of wonders, the howling did gradually get quieter. The Italian engineers had not only stuffed the toilet paper round the door they had also soaked the paper in water so that as the aircraft gained height and the outside temperature dropped the water froze and almost perfect silence was restored. It worked well… and I have never criticised an Italian aero engineer from that day to this day.

Although we knew we were heading for Nairobi we had no idea at all where any refuelling stops would be. Thundering on through the night we slept as best we could and eventually became aware that the nose of the aircraft was pointing earthwards. Soon the bagpipes introduced the Captain who informed us that we were in fact on our way to Aden and would be arriving in the middle of the night – local time.

At the time Aden was probably the one place on earth that no member of the human race would want to visit, let alone a hundred of them fast approaching in an aluminium tube. Rebel forces were making life very difficult for the resident British armed forces and lives were being lost weekly. Of all the places we could have gone for fuel 'Why on earth Aden?' was the cry that echoed from seat to seat as sleep was rubbed from eyes and seat belts fastened in readiness for landing.

Feathering back the props the pilot eased the plane over the threshold of Khormaksar military airfield. With all passengers' eyes scanning fast- approaching lights of all shapes and sizes we were soon back on mother earth and racing down the runway. In a well-practised manoeuvre the aircraft slowed to an appropriate speed to head for the arrivals building, but as it did so armoured personnel carriers appeared from the darkness and escorted the plane to a distant dispersal – well away from the normal arrivals area.

At last the engines were silenced, huge dust clouds generated by the landing started to die away and the doors opened. A blast of hot humid air rushed into the cabin. We could hear the unmistakable and somewhat alarming sound of gunfire – seemingly nearby. There was no 'Welcome to Aden' announcement over the tannoy but that was due to the fact that strong passenger representations to the Captain himself had resulted in a much-reduced number of announcements throughout the night. Mutiny was on hold – for a while…

We were hoarded off the plane and, escorted by heavily armed British troops; we quickly scurried into a large camouflaged marquee erected at the side of the runway. The troops took up defensive positions round our aircraft and we were offered cool drinks to take our minds off the gunfire we could still hear from somewhere behind us.

Ground crews scurried round like bees round a honey pot and thankfully our stay on the ground was to be minimal. Fuel was soon flowing into the aircraft's tanks and even before the operation had been completed we were ushered back onboard and were buckling ourselves in as the fuel lines were removed. In just a few minutes indeed we were airborne again – a very slick operation well carried out. It was a good feeling to be out of the place, even though we had not even seen it. We had tanks full of fuel, the air conditioning was bringing the temperature in the cabin back to something much more acceptable as we settled down for the final leg to Nairobi. We grabbed a few more hours' sleep as the whispering giant ploughed on into a rapidly lightening sky.

We shook ourselves awake as the nose of the plane headed gently down for the last time. Only two announcements from 'Scotland's only…', but what was this - had I been led astray during my geography lessons at school? Looking out of the tiny aircraft windows as the sun came up in glorious fashion – there was the sea. Nairobi and the sea were not together on any map, surely? What on earth was going on now?

The Captain came on the intercom apologising for the 'somewhat different' flight and as we were running 'a few days' late, it seemed, he had taken it on himself to deliver his human cargo to Mombasa, where the great ARK ROYAL lay waiting for her new influx of crew members.

Port Reitz airport, on the outskirts of Mombasa was, in those days, a very small airport indeed and certainly not built for aircraft the size of the Britannia. However, with urgent human cargo onboard our pilot made one run over the airport to take a look and then round again to land at the end of the tiny strip. It says something for the aircraft or pilot or reverse thrust that somehow or other we came to a shuddering halt even after the tarmac of the runway had run out. Hard packed clay produced clouds of dust from under the plane's tyres as local children ran from their mud huts to see this huge early morning noisy 'bird' that had just arrived near, very near, their shanty town village.

We had arrived in sunny Mombasa – still clutching our rail tickets from Nairobi!

CHAPTER THIRTEEN

THE GREAT ARK ROYAL

As the sun rose over tiny Port Reitz airport in Mombasa the huge Britannia dominated the airport buildings, swiftly disgorging its human cargo into the spice-laden atmosphere of a beautiful East African morning. A somewhat bleary eyed, sweaty group of unshaven sailors were hustled through customs and immigration (without any inspections) to our buses as the aircraft prepared to continue its flight south to begin its new role flying fuel, in pitifully small quantities, into landlocked Zambia.

Although we were jaded and badly in need of a refreshing shower and change of clothes, as we arrived at the Kilindini landing stage we could not but fail to be impressed by the huge imposing profile of the ARK ROYAL dominating the beautiful African harbour where she lay at buoys. I thought how many thousands of tons larger she was than the tiny frigate I had left in Scotland a week earlier. It was a wonderful sight in the soft early morning sunlight.

We completed the last leg of our marathon journey lugging suitcases and kit bags up the massive ladders from the small harbour launch that had taken us to the ship, well before anyone was around for the start of another working day. Naturally, my days at Dartmouth were far from my mind, but who was to greet me at the top of the gangway? None other than the Petty Officer Gunnery Instructor who had made my life such a total misery on that wind and snow swept parade ground at Dartmouth just a few years earlier. Life for him, it transpired, had not been all it was cracked up to be as a civilian in the 'outside' world and our little expert in parade training and gunnery skills had not been eagerly sought after by the employers of the South West of England. He had thus rejoined the Navy and shortly after getting his new issue of uniforms and identity card found himself with orders to join the ARK ROYAL in the Far East! Just a short while later he found himself at the top of the gangway just after sunrise to await my arrival - his new boss arriving from the UK! He looked a worried man as he gave me the smartest salute possible, rendering me almost a formal welcome to the mighty Ark and whisked my suitcases away as we headed off to find my new cabin. Far more senior officers watched in amazement, and then carried their own bags off from the boat bay area and into the main body of the ship.

Up ladders and along passage ways... on... and on... this was some huge ship. My man dropped my bags, wished me well and indicated we would be meeting later. He still had a worried look on his face!

My cabin was to be a laughingly-called 'executive suite' on Two deck, just under the flight deck and almost at the stern of the ship. Four junior officers were allocated the space that, we were told six pigs under the then Ministry of Agriculture regulations should be allocated?

Whatever, it was a lot better than the sleeping arrangements we had 'enjoyed' for the past few days. It was now time to get one's bearings of this, my huge new home...

The ship had been lying at Mombasa awaiting its influx of fresh crew members and new orders in the rapidly deteriorating Rhodesian political situation as British leaders met to discuss how the implications of the then Prime Minister Ian Smith's Unilateral Declaration of Independence would be handled.

Within a very few days the ship slipped its huge mooring chains from the harbour buoys and headed out into the Indian Ocean past the magnificent surf breaking over the coral either side of the harbour entrance. Having just about located my eating and sleeping quarters it was time to think about work. I needed a guide to take me to the Bridge many decks above. It was a very long trip.

Having just left a tiny frigate bouncing around off the Icelandic coast I had indeed arrived in ARK ROYAL with a watchkeeping ticket – but the ink on it was hardly dry so I was preparing for a steep learning curve! My experience on the bridge of one of Her Majesty's ships – in sole charge – could be counted in hours, not even days let alone weeks. The only interest of my fellow watchkeepers was whether I had the necessary 'ticket' or not. I had, so there was no debate - I was on the roster! I found my way to the bridge at the appointed hour expecting to find the officer I was, in my opinion, to understudy on this huge 40,000-ton ship. He didn't exist! I was on my own... Talk about being thrown in at the deep end!

Heading out into the glassy calm Indian Ocean with just the hint of a gentle swell the whole ship's company knew we were heading for Singapore many days' steaming away... or thought they did! I had to pinch myself that I was indeed standing on the bridge of Britain's mightiest warship – responsible for some 2000 men onboard – but had yet to celebrate my 21st birthday. If I hadn't realised it before I did now, the Royal Navy give their young officers responsibility at a very early age. I can't pretend I felt relaxed as a fellow officer gave me the 'quick Cook's tour' of all the intercoms, instrumentation and essential equipment on the bridge perched over 80 feet above the sea. He then disappeared below.

To starboard was a superb vista of the sparkling Indian Ocean stretching for many miles to the horizon. To port, the vast flight deck spread out with the flight deck crews scurrying around a mix of Scimitar, Sea Vixen and Gannet aircraft and a squadron of Wessex helicopters parked on deck. Hundreds of sailors were enjoying the early evening air around the aviator's hardware. Having had their evening meal and shower and a very welcome change into clean shorts and a shirt scores of men walked the lengthy flight deck, many clutching a bright plastic mug of tea as they took some gentle exercise after a day working below decks. Not exactly a P&O cruise, but for many of them the only chance they would ever have of experiencing the Indian Ocean coast in all its beauty. For me it was simply immeasurably better than the North Atlantic I had just left behind!

Looking down on the scene from three decks above the flight deck I was beginning to feel almost at home. I had discovered that my Captain – the much respected Michael Fell – was resting his eyelids in his sea cabin just feet behind the compass platform should any crisis arise and that gave me a great feeling of security.

Literally, within the first hour of the watch a signal arrived on the bridge that was to have a major impact on the ship and her ships company for many months to come. It simply said that Her Majesty's government had decided to instigate a blockade of the port of Beira far to the south of us in Mozambique to prevent oil flowing into Rhodesia. ARK ROYAL was to divert and instigate the patrol. It was obviously not a signal totally unexpected by the Captain as he appeared on the bridge. He too had been following events in southern Africa as they unfolded over the BBC World service. My very first helm order on the bridge of that ship was about to be given to the helmsmen many decks below. The simple order of 'Starboard fifteen' was given... we were no longer heading for Singapore as the mighty ship turned gently to starboard leaving a huge curving wake – the only visible sign, for many miles astern, that the Ark had passed by. Within a few minutes our bow was heading south for the Mozambique Channel, to instigate what was to become the 'Beira Patrol'. It was to be a momentous day – and from that point, the months would turn into some nine years before that patrol ended. Many ships and aircraft would be involved, enormous expenditure would be made and lives would be lost. But none of that was of course known on that very first day.

As the engineers eased more steam into the turbines in the engine rooms below the miles were soon eaten up and the East African coast soon slipped by. We were off the long flat coast of Mozambique and the port of Beira just a few days later.

The orders from the UK were simple – no fuel was to reach Rhodesia via the oil pipeline that ran from the port of Beira in Portuguese ruled Mozambique into fuel-starved Rhodesia. We were to 'use all facilities available to us' to stop any shipping heading for the port. With a squadron of Scimitar jets and another of Sea Vixens it was going to be a brave – or stupid – tanker skipper who disregarded the UN backed instructions for all shipping to avoid the port. The seas were empty as we arrived but enormous efforts were already being put into locating anything that remotely resembled an oil tanker. Round the clock, Gannet airborne early-warning aircraft would be punched off the flight deck into the vast and lonely skies. Hour after hour their radars hunted for any sign of shipping hundreds of miles from the ship before they themselves would retrace their steps and start looking for their home; suddenly a huge aircraft carrier would become very much the nautical equivalent of the needle in the haystack. On reporting a contact more often than not a couple of jets would thunder off the decks to locate and identify the vessel, frequently to simply over fly the unsuspecting vessel which would see little more than a friendly 'waggle' of its wings but with a fine armoury of weapons on display on those wings, for use 'if required'.

For the bridge team not a lot changed – one patch of the Indian Ocean looked very much like any other so one watch soon became very similar to another. Normally every watch would see aircraft launched and recovered… hours ran into days as huge areas were searched and sanitised day after day. No ship would pass….

The only noticeable physical difference on the bridge was the installation in those pre-satellite days of a very standard but very red GPO telephone on a bracket right in the centre of the bridge. It just sat… it never rang over the weeks but we had secret instructions onboard that, should we ever find a suspect ship, the red phone would take us to the very inner offices of the Foreign Office in London. We were assured that, on our producing just the name and registry of any suspect vessel, instructions would be issued to either let the ship pass or for it to be blasted from the ocean by the Navy's best pilots – or any such appropriate action in between. On the bridge our instructions were simple – if we used the phone we were just to go through some basic steps the nominated operators would take us through but, secret of all secrets, we had a London phone number pencilled in the back of the deck log that we were to request and ' suitable instructions would be given'. But the tankers never appeared... so none of the Officers who kept those first watches in the early weeks of the patrol ever had cause to make the call.

But then it happened... one Sunday lunchtime a ship was spotted heading our way. Our aircraft reported back its name and port of registry and suddenly it was time to make THE call back to the UK! The Captain appeared on the bridge for this solemn but exciting moment.

As the navigator gingerly approached the handset that we had all looked at for weeks, I asked myself could it really be time after such a wait to pick it up? The navigator did so and almost instantly a deep African voice simply said 'Nairobi' over the intercom on the bridge. Between us we checked the instructions. We were to ask for Rome – so we did. 'Roma,' said the shrill lady's voice just as quickly as had the African operator. Checking the list again, 'Portishead please,' was the request and again within seconds a good heart-warming English voice with a reassuring Bristolian accent was on the line simply saying, 'Portishead – can I help?' It was at this stage we were empowered to ask for the secret number scribbled in the back of the deck log.

Checking for spies over our shoulders in true James Bond fashion the whole bridge team ascertained we were not being followed or our conversation monitored. Thinking of Queen and country the navigator said, 'Can I have London 01... please.' We could all easily hear the operator dialling out the number requested. The tension mounted...

The reply to the Indian Ocean would soon be with us – what would be the fate of this ship and her crew? Then it came... the line clicked and a clear female but doubtless recorded voice told us from so far away... 'Sorry caller... all lines from Bristol are engaged... please try later.'

CHAPTER FOURTEEN

CRASH

The patrol went on for a few more weeks until we were relieved of our duties by the other RN aircraft carrier in the Far East at that time – HMS EAGLE.

After a trip across the Indian Ocean to Singapore, it was to be my first visit to that great city in the difficult days of confrontation with Indonesia. There was plenty to keep a wide-eyed young officer amused during a maintenance period for the ship and her men. Before long however, suitably rested with lockers full of children's toys for the crew's children back in UK, it was time to go back to sea again across the Indian Ocean and head for another Beira patrol.

Once again days stretched into weeks but the politicians said the job had to be done… Gannet aircraft were launched to scour the oceans from high above the clouds (normally at around 8,000ft), again searching for any shipping out to 180 miles from the plane and its ever-searching radar. When a ship was spotted it was the same routine - a radio report was sent back to the mighty Ark and off would fly a Scimitar or Sea Vixen to identify the Gannet's radar contact… and so it went, on and on, day in, day out round the clock.

It was a day's flying just like any other, as sortie after sortie were flown by day and night. After the initial apprehension of standing a watch on my own on the Navy's largest ship just weeks earlier it was, by now, simply routine. Bringing the huge ship into wind just as the aircraft were ready to launch (to give them the maximum wind over the deck for take off) was the necessary skill and co-operation required by the bridge and Flyco (Flying Control position adjacent to the bridge overhanging the flight deck) teams. It was then necessary to bring the ship back to the intended course as soon as the aircraft were airborne.

Piloted by Lieutenant Alan Tarver with a six foot gentle giant of a man by the name of Lieutenant John Stutchbury as the Observer (Navigator) the Sea Vixen roared off the end of the flight deck with the added boost of the Steam catapult to get its lumbering twenty three tons into the morning sky. It started as just another sortie…

On the bridge we carried out our normal navigational duties but the Captain always had one loudspeaker of the many on the bridge tuned into the aircraft frequencies. The chatter between aircraft and their controllers onboard just feet below in the ship's Operations' room was a normal background noise amongst many others that had to be monitored on the bridge.

As the forenoon watch ticked by it became obvious the Vixen was in trouble… the background noise of the chatter between aircraft and onboard controller was suddenly no longer considered background – all ears were strained as the pilot reported a major loss of fuel. A standby Scimitar tanker aircraft was always kept on deck ready for such an emergency (recent history had dictated that it was often necessary) and within a very few minutes it was airborne and heading skywards for the crippled Vixen. Soon we were hearing the chatter between the two pilots on our bridge speaker. The whole bridge crew froze as they listened to the drama unfolding. As the Scimitar arrived on the scene Vixen pilot Alan Tarver, flying his powerless aircraft as a glider, did his best to get the refuelling probe mounted on the wing of his aircraft into the basket attached to the fuelling hose leading from the belly of the tanker. As the Vixen was literally falling from the sky with no power it was a hopeless task. No fuel was ever to pass between the Scimitar and Sea Vixen. The Scimitar eventually could only circle the fast developing situation and report back on the unfolding crisis. All thoughts of taking fuel onboard had been forgotten.

The speaker crackled into life as the Vixen pilot told his observer to abandon the aircraft – by ejector seat. For some reason his hi-tech seat, which should have blasted him well clear of the aircraft, simply didn't work…. the doomed plane continued to fall. The pilot then instructed his observer to jettison the canopy over his head and, in a superb piece of flying he inverted his plane in an attempt to drop his observer, still in his seat, free. I will never forget the pilot's words over his intercom as he said to his fellow crew member, 'John, I'll get you out of here if it kills me,' in the calmest of voices as the plane headed ever groundwards. It very nearly did just that, as his observer was unable to drop or crawl out of his 'coal hole' (behind and to the side of the pilot) for seemingly no other reason than he was over 6ft tall. From the story being recounted back to the ship it was obvious he had managed to get half out of what was to be his fast-descending coffin but the slipstream had him pinned back against the fuselage of the plane...

In one last desperate attempt to shake his buddy free Tarver managed to invert the powerless aircraft still falling all the time. It was his last hope... the sea was fast approaching.

The six-footer remained stuck by his heavy flying boots laid back on the fuselage of the plane. None of us on the bridge could see anything but we could all visualise the situation just hundreds of feet above us – we were getting an excellent word picture from the Scimitar pilot above coming through the speakers nearby – as we looked at similar aircraft ranged on the deck below us.

By now Tarver had only seconds to save his own life. His aircraft was on its side as he, at what was well past the last minute, pulled his own ejection seat handle above his head. The normal emergency ejection method is expected to take place when a plane is flying more or less straight and level. On pulling the ejection strop above his head the pilot and his seat are hurled through the canopy and seconds later both automatically separate. If all goes to plan a parachute deploys to bring the lucky aviator slowly back to the ground, or sea, below. Alan Tarver, however, was hurled horizontally away from the plane and hit the sea a glancing blow – doubtless bouncing more than once along the surface. It was however only a short while before the Search and Rescue helicopter, already airborne, was hovering above him and he was whisked back to the ship's deck. His face in particular was not a pretty sight and he was unable to walk; yet against all the odds, after such a low and dangerous sideways ejection, he was alive! (He was later awarded the George Medal for his heroic attempt to save his observers life).

As the bridge intercom went completely silent the Vixen with John Stutchbury still pinned to the fuselage had ploughed into the sea a few miles from the ship just out of sight. There was total silence everywhere. We all knew the outcome. Although we understood it was a totally hopeless task we still spent many an hour looking for the unfortunate observer – but no evidence of him or the tiniest part of his plane was ever located.

As the day went on it was time to resume operations. The plan was to get every airworthy plane airborne to get every available pilot flying as soon as possible. They had to concentrate on their flying, not focus on their lost colleague and friend. All was not all over however – it was to be a bad day in the flying pro-gramme as another aircraft, a Gannet, had an accident on landing, after dark, and shot straight over the port side of the ship. Was I a Jonah onboard, I wondered, as once again I was the officer of the watch and witnessed the whole event? As, it later transpired, the forward nose wheel and assembly collapsed or hadn't been lowered properly and the aircraft careered along the deck, its two propellers beat-ing at the massively thick steel deck (reputed to be some ten inches thick) of the ARK. Being so thick no damage was done to the deck but for the aircraft it was quite another story! Fortunately it floated briefly and all the crew were safely recovered – found sitting on the sinking fuselage as help arrived.

What a day!

CHAPTER FIFTEEN

CAMELS AHOY

Throughout the long days of the Beira patrols numerous 'bright ideas' were instigated to keep morale up, none longer running than a proposed camel trek through Egypt. Everyone on board was told that during the ship's forthcoming northbound transit of the Suez canal the British Naval Attaché in Cairo could book a group of camels for a team of lucky sailors to trek up the canal at the same time as the ship proceeded north. Copies of signals to the Naval attaché were left in conspicuous parts of the ship and a note inserted in the ship's Daily Orders solicited sailors interested in getting off the ship for a few days to apply for a place on 'the great Egyptian camel trek – the trip of a lifetime.' Ship's officers were deluged with officially completed 'request chits' from their sailors seeking the opportunity to escape the ship and mount up.

ARK ROYAL had one of the earliest TV stations on board one of Her Majesty's ships. A redundant, long, thin compartment was taken over by the budding programme makers. A single camera was mounted in the centre of the compartment and swung wildly between interviewer and interviewee at either end of the compartment as locally made programmes unfolded. It was all very amateur but viewing figures were high. Of all the output that came from Ark TV a much appreciated current affairs programme screened live every Monday was essential viewing. With the same transmission time as its BBC TV Panorama clone at home, came locally produced 'PanArkorama' to every TV monitor onboard.

Starting at 2000 but ending at any time at all, the programme gave both serious and many far less serious current affairs items an airing throughout the ship. It was indeed compulsive viewing on a Monday night!

PanArkorama was chosen as the best method to promote and brief the potential camel trekkers. The first job was to select the fortunate twenty trekkers from the hundreds of hopefuls who applied. On the appointed programme a huge dustbin was produced full of all the completed Request chits for the much heralded draw to decide who would join the trek. Every one had been talking about it for days. The Captain was persuaded to leave his sea cabin and head for the TV studio deep in the bowels of the ship to conduct the draw. A Padre was persuaded to accompany him to check the draw was conducted without any dubious or doubtful sleight of hand. Before the draw took place the OICCT (Officer in Command – Camel Trekking) gave a full on-screen briefing of the intended trek. This expedition was obviously not for the feint hearted… a ship's phone number was issued on air – in case anyone was having second thoughts and wanted to back out. 'Ring now… drop out… and save any major embarrassment later,' was the TV message passed throughout the ship. Doubtless some did….but there were plenty of people to take their places.

To the accompaniment of two of the ship's Royal Marine bandsmen shoe-horned into the studio with trombone and trumpet (there was no room for more, either men or instruments) the Captain made an appropriate speech -wishing he could be spared for the trek rather than be responsible for the ship's safe passage through the Suez canal.

With much hype and theatre, names were eventually pulled from the dustbin and the presenter of PanArkorama was eventually able to announce the lucky team. As the ship continued its Beira patrol viewers were told to tune in again next week for more news… and so it went on and on – week after week. The selected lucky trekkers were the heroes of the week and walked tall throughout the ship.

As the weeks went by various ship's officers were invited onto the programme to brief the trekkers (with the full knowledge the rest of the ship's company would be watching too). First up was the ship's Principal Medical Officer who required the trekkers to take endless notes re Egyptian diseases that may be encountered, and to announce a timetable for injections for every conceivable illness – known and unknown – throughout the Middle East. Days later a queue could be seen outside the Sick Bay as trekkers waited their turn to be jabbed. They were back a few days later for another appointment with the needle. It seemed that they were being jabbed for every disease known to man.

The following week the ship's PT instructors were on the small screen advising of a suitable pre-trek keep fit routine... they were followed by the ship's Cash officer giving a currency brief and announcing the hours his office would be open to allow trekkers the chance to change their Sterling into US dollars which they were told would be acceptable ashore. (Unfortunately no Egyptian currency was held in the ship's safe.)

By now incoming 'signals' arrived from the British Naval Attaché in Cairo confirming the camels were booked. As the boredom of a Beira patrol continued the camel trek was on everyone's lips. Who cared if tankers carried fuel into Beira or not!

More briefings were required... more instructions from the medics re 'motion sickness' that could be encountered whilst 'on the hump' were given, more pills were offered...

The Padres gave an excellent comprehensive briefing on religious customs and traditions that could be encountered en route... better to be safe than sorry. The trekkers scribbled away in their notebooks as the briefings continued.

The day for the great trek got ever nearer. The last day of the Beira patrol passed as half sister HMS EAGLE arrived to take over again and ARK headed for Aden. I was to spend my 21st birthday there just sweltering on my bunk with the air conditioning struggling to cope with 90degree-plus temperatures – and certainly no leave. Less than a day was spent in this far from hospitable port. We couldn't linger for much more time than was needed to pick up the mail (and most had been sent to Singapore anyway)... there was an urgent date for a camel trek on the horizon.

As we headed up through the shimmering and sweltering waters of the Red Sea photographs of eggs frying on the steel upper deck were taken to impress the folks back home in a few weeks time.

On leaving Aden more briefings were needed... the ship's Bosun was produced with a length of 'genuine Egyptian cotton rope' to explain how to bind up the front left leg of a camel to make a useful step to enable the rider to mount the beast. It was all beginning to sound just a little silly and a touch far fetched... but the briefings conducted without the hint of a smile.

Days later the ship's navigator was interviewed along with the senior engineer. How would the trekkers navigate their ships of the desert, was the briefing of the day. 'Special' frequencies were issued for the trekkers to note in their bulging briefing books. They learnt that at fixed hours of the day the ship would transmit on these 'special' frequencies and, using a 'special' black box that would be given to the trekkers when they started their adventure, navigation would be possible. As the ship transited the canal out of sight, the special black box held at arm's length and passed through 180 degrees from the body would give a massive jolt to the operator when he passed it through the bearing on which the ship lay. It would feel uncomfortable but at least it would be impossible to get lost!

An 'emergency' arrangement was also announced whereby every half hour the ship's boiler room crew would make a huge pall of black smoke (they were always good at it – normally just as the ship entered the critical phase of landing aircraft). Again the trekkers would see the black mushroom clouds popping up as the ship progressed up the canal. There would be no biblical star to follow into Egypt, just black oil sodden man-made clouds up above the canal.

It was a very gullible sailor indeed who by this stage (just a single day's steaming south of the canal entrance) hadn't realised he had been 'had' by a very complex spoof. It had run for weeks… it had certainly given hundreds of very bored officers and men a talking point. Some very red-faced sailors were to be seen the next day, arms punctured with unknown vaccines, pockets full of unnecessary US dollars but well versed in local Egyptian customs about the ship. All well prepared, but not a camel in sight. They took it well – to a man. They could do little else!

But the last laugh? As the ship eased its way towards the entrance of the canal itself hundreds of men appeared on the flight deck to witness the rare sight of such a huge ship squeezing itself into the canal. Much film was expended – it was definitely to be one for the family album. As the officer of the watch as we approached the canal my eye fell towards a blur in the heat haze on the canal bank whilst we were still someway off. We slowly completed the last mile to the canal entrance and it was obvious the 'blur' was in fact at least two dozen camels feeding by the canal side.

It was too good an opportunity to miss… the captain readily agreed for an announcement to be made on all the ship's internal and external flight deck loudspeakers.

In his best 'official' voice the bosun's mate announced to the entire ship's company, 'Those ratings proceeding on the camel trek muster in the starboard boat bay in five minutes' time – the camels are now in attendance.'

I can only guess the reaction of the men below decks but the hundreds on the flight deck turned to look up at the bridge – from where they knew the announcement emanated. As their jaws sagged a little and a quizzical look spread across their faces the ship slowly entered the famous canal leaving the camels grazing just a few yards away.

We had all enjoyed the last editions of PanArkorama East of Suez.

CHAPTER SIXTEEN

JUST A QUIET POSTCARD RUN

The decision had been made, after so many months at sea, that ARK was to enter the port of Gibraltar for some rest and relaxation before returning to the UK. With pockets bulging with many an unopened pay packet that they had been unable to spend for so long 'the boys' were going to be let loose on the unsuspecting residents of the Rock. The word on board was that they needed somewhere to 'unwind' before getting back to Devonport.

Just forty-eight hours was allocated for a run ashore in Gibraltar to buy a few last minute presents and the obligatory post cards. Half the ship's company were to be given the first day in harbour off, the other half were to have the second day ashore, and then it was to be homeward bound.

Whilst the chairman of the Chamber of Commerce and his opposite number at the local publican's organisation doubtless started rubbing their hands with glee at the thought of two thousand new customers being deposited on their doorstep – with many months of pay in their wallets and no previous opportunity to spend it – the local police, both military and civilian, doubtless started to worry at the size of the problem they could have!

As expected, the ship's company stormed ashore minutes after the ship's arrival – the first time the berthing ropes had been used onboard since leaving Singapore many months earlier. Sailors literally streamed down the gangway like a plague of locust descending on an unsuspecting field of crops. It was definitely time to catch up on some shopping, but also for a very considerable number of people to get their first pint of Watneys Red barrel (flavour of the month at that time) after long months abroad and having had their palette tainted by Singapore's Tiger beer (of which the ship still held hundreds of crates in the store rooms below decks).

On the first night in harbour I was rostered to be the Officer of the Watch on the gangway from 0400.Watches at sea were fine but in harbour it was a duty only required on ships the size of a carrier and never popular with junior naval officers – but there were enough of them onboard so the duty didn't come round too frequently. Normally the greatest excitement of a watch at that time of day was to witness the sunrise – always an awe-inspiring sight – and to get the first bacon sandwich and cup of tea of a new day inside one's bored and tired body.

But this morning watch was to be 'somewhat different'. On arriving in the starboard forward boat bay into which the huge gangway from the jetty was secured my predecessor was visibly fatigued. He had been kept going for the previous four hours since midnight by a stream of drunks, semi drunks and very, very drunks. He showed me a bathroom nearby and the whole of the huge compartment was not a pretty sight. That night the rules for determining drunkenness ere simple: if someone walked onboard they were classified as being sober and allowed to proceed to their messdeck (a very lucky classification for many). However, if they had to be brought onboard over a mate's shoulder or by any other means they were 'officially' drunk. As such, they were laid out on the deck of the bathroom – frequently in their best Burton's civilian suit. It is unnecessary to describe the scene in great detail as some sixty or more matelots made complete fools of themselves. A sailor on duty nearby with a fire hose was also useful when any of the suffering souls wanted to start a singsong – or stand up and return to their messdeck. The salt water from the hose at full pressure was enough to have the most adventurous matelot back in his temporary messdeck – with the emphasis very much on the word 'mess' too! You don't need the details.

The bathroom was not a pretty sight, nor was it a particularly safe place to be. With so many men in such a poor state it could have led to a real problem; anyone in such a state can easily drown in their own vomit, or choke. Until this point in my life I thought 'A Night To Remember' was just the name of a film – I was rapidly learning otherwise.

Leaving the incumbents of the bathroom to the safety of a couple of their messmates to keep an eye on them (what a great job) and the stoker with his fire hose,

I returned to the gangway to be responsible for whatever was to occur over the next four hours. By the number of people coming and going it could have been four in the afternoon not in the morning. A constant stream of sailors returned from their run ashore as the clock slowly headed towards dawn. I mused that only milkmen should be up working at this time of the day...

As I sipped my first cuppa of the day my attention was drawn to a taxi as it drew up at the bottom of the gangway with seemingly only the driver in it. As it stopped, the driver hopped out... pulled a very dishevelled heap out from the back seat... dumped him at the base of the gangway and sped off into the night. This was undoubtedly the busiest night of the Gibraltar taxi drivers' year and not a minute could be wasted!

Of the three of us in the boat bay at that time our reaction was all the same – we surely had one dead sailor on our hands. As two of us rushed down the huge forty foot gangway our 'body' made some very minimal movements so we were happy life had not totally left him. We returned to our duties reminding ourselves that if he walked onboard he was sober, should he crawl he was drunk... He must have known the rules that night, as he was absolutely determined he was going to walk onboard – even if it took a while.

After the first hour he had indeed got to his feet and by taking assistance offered by other sailors returning onboard had climbed the eighteen inches up onto the front of the huge steel gangway itself.

For most of the second hour his time was spent clutching the gangway handrail, taking two steps forward and then one back again. He was in no hurry to get to his bunk and chatted to his passing messmates as they headed home at a far faster pace.

As he approached those of us in the 'welcoming party' at the top of the gangway and as the sun started to appear I noticed that in each pocket was a bottle of what looked like cheap Spanish red wine. How they had not been broken as he made his fast exit from the taxi, I know not; the Spanish obviously use tough bottles for their wines.

Any form of alcohol was strictly forbidden for junior sailors onboard, which is why they took to the juice with such fervent interest when ashore. There was no way the bottles in 'gangwayman's' pockets were coming onboard but my mind was still open as to whether he was drunk or sober. He had been on his feet for the last two hours but progress was still best described as 'somewhat slow'.

113

As the watch ticked by, innumerable routines were carried out around the boat bay and gangway area... it would soon be time to 'call the hands' over the tannoy and another day would soon be underway. Who knew 'gangwayman' might not even be onboard before leave expired at 0730. His progress was that slow.

Eventually he made it to the very top rung of the gangway. Beaming from ear to ear with success he stood there to appreciate and savour the moment. I stood right in front of him blocking any further movement forward onto the ship. Trying hard not to smile I congratulated him on his efforts to return to his ship but had to ask what he had in each pocket.

'Tew bottles of Weeskey, suur...' he managed to say. The bottles remained in his very crumpled suit pocket but they were, as I suspected, cheap Spanish red wine. He had doubtless made a somewhat 'incorrect purchase' somewhere ashore that evening...

Whilst not actually thanking him for helping our watch pass quickly I stood to my full height and in my best 'official' voice said that whilst we had all enjoyed the sight of his return to the ship there was no way I was going to allow the booze, whatever it was, onboard. I said that I would walk the thirty feet to the end of the boat bay and, if I heard two good splashes he could indeed come onboard – and no more would be said. He could then be classified as being 'sober'.

It was at this point he fell on my neck from his higher position on the gangway... I'm sure he attempted to kiss me... mumbled on and on that he always knew I was the best officer they had on the ship... and that he would be taking me ashore with him the next night as he had found this wonderful girl ashore who would be just right for me...

Fighting away his amorous advances we agreed that the noise of the two splashes would be his audio passport to return onboard.

The agreement made... hands were for some reason, eventually, shaken and I walked down the thirty feet of the boat bay.

Within seconds of leaving 'gangwayman' I heard the splashes I wanted to hear. I returned to the gangway itself quietly congratulating myself that I had handled this delicate situation well... another 'incident' resolved... only to see our man still upright on the gangway, still with his red wine in his pocket..... but no shoes on his feet!

CHAPTER SEVENTEEN

HOME FROM THE SEA

The ARK eventually managed to leave Gibraltar but also left some sailors behind, to explain to the magistrates their activities whilst ashore over the previous 48 hours. A task far easier I would imagine than explaining to the wife or girlfriend in UK who they were expecting to meet on the jetty in Devonport a few days later! Enormous quantities of presents had been purchased for loved ones back home from the shops in Main Street... the gangway was eventually removed, tugs eased the 40,000 ton ship away from the jetty and soon the huge screws were turning once again to get the ship heading back to Devonport just a few days steaming over the final 1,000 miles of the deployment.

For any ship and many generations of sailors the passing of Plymouth breakwater and steaming up the last few miles into the naval base has always been an emotive moment. This day was to be no different. Families had come from all over the UK to welcome their men folk home. 'Welcome Home' banners were waved frantically ashore as small children peered at the huge ship passing in the early morning mist looking for their dad whom they hadn't seen for so many months. As the Royal Marine band assembled on the jetty to welcome the ship home I was in the shower watching the Devon scenery passing through the scuttle (porthole). As a relatively new boy to the ship and also as someone who had no wife or girlfriend on the jetty to meet him it was fairly obvious who was going to do the first gangway watch as the Harbour Officer of the Watch that morning.

Complete with traditional telescope (it didn't work and the 'eye piece' was removable to reveal a suitable compartment with screw cap top in which it had been known for some officers to conceal a tot of something appropriate to keep their spirits up through the long night watches), it would soon be time to see fair play at the top of the gangway as streams of officers and men made their way ashore on leave whilst, in the opposite direction, another stream saw endless families pouring onboard to seek out their men folk.

It was an emotional time for most. Many men onboard would say they had been homesick onboard for the long Far East Commission: ARK was their home - and they were sick of it. Living conditions for some onboard were far from the best, even by 1960 standards; some men didn't even have a bunk and locker - they only had a camp bed and a suitcase. Not exactly what they had expected from the recruiting literature of the day.

As the crowds on the quarterdeck started to thin out as families found their men folk and followed them back to their messdecks to 'see where daddy has been living' I was left with an ever diminishing crowd on the ceremonial quarterdeck. Eventually I was left with just one young mum plus a very excited three year old looking for his dad. Offering to help, I found out who the appropriate dad was and phoned through to the Engine Room department to see if he was, as I expected, on duty way below shutting machinery down that wouldn't be used for many a week. He wasn't. As the three year old was in danger of doing something very silly in his excitement and frustration of not having his dad to hand I eventually tracked the missing father down by phone – a senior rating – in his mess where my phone calls found him drinking beer. On advising him that his wife and young child were waiting for him on the quarterdeck he made it very clear that he was having a beer with his mates and when he had finished he would come and meet his family. Had I been able to leave my place of duty for much longer I would have stormed into his mess and physically frog-marched him down to meet his next of kin – even though that wasn't exactly what my duties that morning should have included. Both wife and son deserved far better treatment whatever the state of their relationship.

How do you tell an over excited three year old that dad found a glass of beer with his mates more important than meeting his son whom he hadn't seen for many months? Eventually he sauntered onto the quarterdeck – in his overalls - and took his family away but it didn't need a trained social worker to assess the long-term viability of that particular marriage. Unfortunately, as many sailors know, the seagoing life is not always the best for marriages – or regretfully, three year olds.

116

After weeks alongside giving leave to the ships company it was time to embark on the final few months of the ship's life before entering a major refit at Devonport. We were soon heading for Portsmouth to 'star' as the main attraction at the local Navy Days where the public were encouraged to 'See the ships and meet the men' they were funding as taxpayers. The public needed little encouragement. For three days over the bank holiday the ship's many gangways were packed with members of the public eager to explore every nook and cranny of the Navy's largest warship.

At 1800 when the last member of the public, the last family and final small child had left the ship it was time to relax a little. Having done my stint answering questions from the public, letting families take photos of young Jimmy alongside a real Navy Officer with Jimmy proudly posing with the telescope under his arm, I felt very sorry for servicemen such as those who mount the Guard on Horseguards parade each day. Dealing with the public is hard work...

I chose to retire to see my friend Tony Barber (from Malta minesweeping days) who by now was a Submariner and closing his submarine down for the night, it too having been open to the public just astern of the ARK.

Enjoying some suitable 'Navy Days medicine' in his wardroom our peace was disturbed by a huge sailor who appeared in the tiny doorway of the pig shed (as the wardroom was unkindly known by junior ratings). He held an up-turned sailor's cap under his arm. It looked strangely bulging and heavy...

Inquiring what he wanted he didn't reply but simply stepped forward and, turning the sailor's cap over proceeded to pour the contents all over the table and deck of the wardroom. Coins bounced everywhere. Surrounded by hundreds of coins of the realm my friend inquired, not unnaturally, what was going on. Our burly sailor friend simply replied, 'That's your share, Sir...' and disappeared back behind the curtain into the passageway outside.

As I started to pick up the coins my chum left in haste to catch the aforementioned sailor to see why we were suddenly deluged with small change. I was still collecting and counting them when he returned to explain that 'using his initiative' (ah, that familiar Dartmouth phrase yet again!) he and the fellow members of the duty watch had simply placed an upturned sailor's hat with a few coins in it at the top of the hatch exactly where a constant stream of visitors emerged back into daylight and the real world after probably their first viewing of the cramped interior of one of Her Majesty's submarines. Emerging from the torpedo-loading hatch visitors were obviously amazed that anyone would volunteer to serve Queen and Country by going to sea in such an inhospitable vessel. The up turned sailor's cap had an effect similar to that of the Poppy seller, RNLI fund-raising lifeboat on a pub bar or the door-to-door collector for the NSPCC. You have to be a pretty hard soul to pass them by... the submariners that day reported they had to empty the hat no less than three times and the pile of coins now spilling onto the wardroom deck was the Officer of the Day's 'share'. No one actually counted the cash, they simply grabbed a galley ladle and everyone onboard on duty that day had two generous ladles full – just for using their initiative!

The ARK's next mission was to lead a British task group in a major NATO exercise off the North of Scotland, in which the mighty Soviet Navy took a very close interest – as they did in those days.

With the exercise behind us we were programmed to make an official visit to the beautiful Norwegian capital of Oslo. To be able to visit Oslo at the best of times is good; to be taken there on the payroll of the Royal Navy in a major capital ship was fantastic. The Norwegians certainly held the Royal Navy in high esteem and seemingly the whole city went out of it's way to make the ship and her huge crew welcome during the extra long light days of mid summer.

After the visit we wound our way down the beautiful but narrow Oslo Fjord. It was quite a navigational feat but we were soon heading for the open sea and the long awaited dry dock in Devonport for a very long refit. The Norwegians had done us proud – some perhaps too proud, as hangovers were nursed and sleep regained.

As a mere twenty-one year old some readers may doubtless ask if it was right that such a person as I was left alone on the bridge totally responsible for the safe navigation of the ship and the safety of her two thousand crew members below. But it happened as we hurtled towards the Dover straits at almost full power. It must have been some sight from offshore or mid channel viewing the mighty ARK pounding along. In such a situation in coastal waters the Officer of the watch is well used to yachtsmen and cross channel ferries altering course a touch to come and take a closer look; fortunately they could normally be expected to keep at a reasonable distance and not make any silly moves that would endanger everyone.

All was going well – heading on a course for the Dungeness peninsula at a steady twenty-five knots with few radar or visual contacts ahead on a balmy summer Sunday afternoon. I knew I had to make a course alteration to port shortly if I wasn't to steam up Dungeness beach, but two tiny 'specs' were just starting to appear ahead of me on the radar, in exactly the area into which I wanted – indeed had – to turn. Closer investigation through binoculars confirmed the two specs were two small inshore fishing vessels, pair trawling (they were connected by wire and their nets spread between them). They were steaming slowly away from us and their skippers had no reason to look over their shoulders as they slowly dragged their shared net along the seabed. They would doubtless have lost one… possibly more… heartbeats had they done so.

With the sweat beads beginning to form on my forehead a situation was fast developing that was 'above my pay grade'. It was time to call the Captain who I knew was in his sea cabin immediately aft of the bridge. He failed to respond to my first call – or second. On my third attempt as the fishermen came ever closer he acknowledged my call and as if emerging from a deep sleep, enquired if they were bigger than us and then seemed to go back to sleep again. It was time to act as the Kent coast came ever closer right ahead. A gentle turn to port was all that was required and I gave the appropriate orders… we were up to the fishermen by now and I was able to shave past, at speed and very very close, so close in fact that from where I stood on the bridge, offset as it was to starboard, the closest fishermen disappeared totally from view…it was an anxious few moments to watch astern to see the tiny vessel thankfully reappear bobbing wildly in the hefty wake generated by the ship at such a speed.

A much-anticipated visit to Devonport was in the forefront of most people's minds. It would be a long one, as the ship would soon be taken in hand by the dockyard for a major refit to enable her to eventually operate the latest naval aircraft. It was time for the vast majority of the ship's company to leave the mighty ARK. For most it was a period of leave and then a new job ashore – but not for the Navy's junior seamen officers. The sea would soon be calling again.

CHAPTER EIGHTEEN

FROM TRAINEE TO TRAINER

It only seemed months before that I had been a young trainee in the Dartmouth Training Squadron but now I was being sent back as a 'proper' ship's officer in the very same squadron where I had learnt my trade. Surely they didn't need me to pass on words of wisdom to the young officers who had been through Dartmouth in the very short time since I had left the place? Someone must have given me a good report somewhere along the line for me to end up here…

Finding HMS EASTBOURNE in Devonport – a sister ship to my own 'old ship' HMS TENBY just a few years earlier – wasn't too difficult. She was preparing to set out on one of her regular three month long voyages to train young officers in the ways of the sea and the Royal Navy. The frigate was considered to be an asset to the Fleet, but officers under training filled a considerable number of billets in her scheme of complement - from the Royal Navy and many overseas navies too – it was a good earner for HM Treasury. It was quite a responsibility to have so many totally untrained people onboard and still attempt to operate from time to time as an anti-submarine frigate. The numbers of qualified officers onboard were also reduced; this meant that those in the wardroom had to work particularly hard. Not many naval officers can talk of taking a frigate to sea with just nine officers on board, including the Captain, but we did it. From very early days it was obvious it was going to be a 'work hard/play hard' type of job.

My role (again) as the most junior officer onboard was mainly to watch keep on the bridge for seemingly endless four-hour watches and also to run the ship's office (again) as, despite its size, this frigate carried no Supply Officer to run the Captains office, pay, feed and clothe the crew and make sure all the stores needed were onboard. The First Lieutenant carried out the additional duties needed to feed the ship's company, the Engineer officer took responsibility for stores and spares and I was responsible for the paperwork and pay. In addition, on this particular vessel, from the minute the ship left harbour everyone had an understudy, as young officers fresh out of the classrooms ashore were keen to experience everything going on round about them. Many were destined to be seamen officers so navigation was always a high priority.

The ship had been fitted with four extra chart tables, one just behind the main bridge of the ship and two on top of the ship's large chartroom further aft which, in time of war, could rapidly be converted into a small helicopter hangar. In each of these positions at all times when the ship was at sea a cadet would be beavering away plotting the ship's position onto his chart – using the extra chart tables and gyro compass repeaters fed from the ship's main compass. They had to spend their whole time plotting the ship's position and reporting to the 'real' Officer of the Watch their views and recommendations as to any alterations of course and speed needed to be made to get the ship from one agreed navigational point on the chart to another. Reports would flow in from all four positions (and another from a position below decks in the operations room using only radar data) throughout the watch. Cadets would suggest increases or decreases of speed or alterations of course to enable them to arrive at their end of watch position bang on time and in geographically the right place. It was not unknown however for all five 'bridge' staff to come up with slightly different proposals. There was certainly no excuse for incorrect navigation of that particular ship!

It is interesting to note that those ships in the Dartmouth Squadron were the only vessels in Her Majesty's fleet in which the Officer of the Watch was allowed to actually leave the bridge during his watch. It was 'legal' for him actually to be on top of the chartroom roof supervising the young cadet doing his best at the chart table there. It must be admitted however Cadets seemed to have better supervision on calm sunny days up there than at 0300 on a wet and windy winter's night.

The Mediterranean was to be our normal stamping ground. It seemed our programme was quite flexible; so long as we were at sea from Monday to Friday no one seemed to mind which port we visited at the weekends, just to catch up on our beauty sleep you understand! Gibraltar was a routine stop on entering and leaving the Mediterranean and Malta was a regular stopping off point on at least two or three occasions during each cruise. In between we were to call at a wide range of ports – from Istanbul to Tangier. We never went by any direct route but followed the coastline so that all the budding navigators had plenty of headlands and lighthouses to use to practise accurate coastal navigation.

On my first cruise we had a very high proportion of foreign cadets from mainly African and Middle Eastern nations. Rumour had it that they were sent to EASTBOURNE as she was the only ship in the squadron with stabilisers, a much appreciated piece of equipment by many of them as they were often very prone to seasickness - far worse than I ever experienced.

By day the cadets would prepare their charts with all the information they needed; their start position, and courses to 'way points' en route to their final destination some three or four hours later. From this they could calculate the speed they would need to recommend when they appeared on 'their' bridge during the night.

PREPARATION… PREPARATION… PREPARATION… was drummed into them. The more preparations they could make before going on watch was preferable, as time would fly once they were navigating 'for real'.

Shortly after the start of the cruise the ship was slowly heading down the Italian coast with cadets navigating normally in every available position. The reports were streaming in from all of those on or around the upper deck indicating that the ship was to starboard of track and slightly ahead of the position intended. I was happy they were all right and intended to make a slight correction to the ship's course and speed later in the watch before the next team took over. From below decks however the intercom reported that the ship was both on course and 'just right' for position and speed… For an hour or more I noticed the reports were always the same. Things were reportedly just great.

Unable by the rules to go below decks I decided to invite the cadet on watch in the Ops room to bring his chart and notebooks to the bridge so that I could see what he was up to… A minute later an African stumbled up the ladder to the bridge – dressed in pyjamas and Wellington boots – with his chart rolled up under his arm. It was shortly after 2.30 in the morning.

He spread his chart on my chart table for me to see why his assessment of the navigational situation was so good but opposed to all the other cadets. It was soon clear that not only did he have all his radar fixes on the chart for the period since he came on watch (at midnight). He also had them already drawn on the chart for the next hour. He had obviously drawn them all on before going on watch and was quite happy to sit back on the intercom reporting every twenty minutes that all was well. Gently challenging him that the plan was not to do everything in advance and 'real' data was needed as the watch passed – he retorted, almost scolding me, that the most important thing with coastal navigation was, 'PREPARATION, PREPARATION, PREPARATION!'

Arriving back in Malta was always a pleasurable experience – even in winter. Just the sandstone rocks gave the whole place a warm feel to it and I had become surprisingly attached to the place over the months I had been coming and going from it.

As part of the socialising for which Her Majesty's ships are somewhat renowned the wardroom organised a 'Shipwreck party' whilst the ship spent the weekend close to the naval headquarters at Fort St Angelo. As ever, guests were invited from the local Wrens establishment at Whitehall Mansions. Care always having to be taken that if Wrens were invited Wren Officers were not. It was a great social 'black' to mix the invites. On this – and many future occasions – it was decided to invite a selection of good old jenny wrens, leaving their officers off the invitation list. History dictates it was normally a good move, as many years later, after many a twist and turn in life's rich and rolling pageant, I married one of these gorgeous young Radar Plotter Wrens that I met for the first time that evening. Although, on that first meeting my main memory is one of persuading my Captain that he should look elsewhere for a suitable shipwrecked mariner that evening. Not an easy or diplomatic task to fulfil for the most junior officer onboard!

Thence to Istanbul...

One of our reasons for visiting Malta had been to collect some 16-year-old trainee seamen from the new entry-training establishment at HMS RALEIGH. They had been flown to Malta from their base in Torpoint, Cornwall, to join EASTBOURNE for their very first taste of life at sea. They were very young, highly impressionable and keen to see all that the Navy, and Istanbul, had to offer. Each day they too were 'farmed out' around the various departments of the ship to see what everyone did on a real ship – as opposed to their only navy experience to date, back in a classroom, ashore in Cornwall.

As we headed towards Istanbul from Malta the temperature dropped dramatically... snow flurries swirled around the bridge as we neared the Bosphorus. Arriving on the bridge at 0400 it was a very routine job to ascertain the position and course of the ship before taking over the watch. It was then a priority for the senior rating of the watch to allocate tasks for the men on duty with him at that time of the morning. Most knew them, having been there so many times before. The only thing that changed was the time of day or night when the duties had to be performed. For the youngsters from RALEIGH it was different – they had to be spoon-fed and everything explained in detail. They were all given various duties from helmsman to lookout and tasked to move on after thirty minutes in each role to give everyone a good look round and to share the jobs during the watch.

A very young, spotty-faced, Liverpudlian was allocated as the starboard lookout. It was explained it was a simple job to keep a good visual look out, from outside the bridge, reporting into the bridge any shipping, lights or other items that he felt may be of interest to me as the Officer of the Watch. As he listened to the huge radars above him whirring round it was explained that although the radar could see far further than his teenage eyes there were frequently things, particularly those close to the ship that the radar would miss. His eyes were important to the safety of the ship. Suitably briefed he stepped outside the warmth of the enclosed bridge into the swirling snow coming off the Turkish coastline a few miles away as the ship headed for an early morning arrival in Istanbul.

The system wasn't foolproof that night… no one had allocated a relief for the youngster and he didn't have the bottle to open the bridge door and seek help. By the time we spotted him nearly four hours later he was in a bad way. "Sir" had told him to stand on the bridge wing and open the door and report any shipping he saw. With no shipping to spot meant he never did open the door. When someone went to the Bridge wing at the change of the watch at 0800 they saw a snowman. Totally white on the top half of his body he was frozen stiff, literally. Rapidly whisked into the warmth of the bridge he was given a short piece of advice on using his initiative in such circumstances and was helped below decks to get something warm inside him. I saw him days later in Istanbul and could swear he was walking in a very stiff manner – I can only assume he was still thawing out.

The three ships of the Squadron anchored in the Bosphorus close to the city centre. It was a fine high profile position. The Turks would certainly know the Royal Navy was in town – especially after dark when the ships were floodlit. It was always a fine sight.

The first day in port was always a busy time for any warship's captain – this day was to be no exception. He would have to chug ashore in the ship's motorboat to pay his respects on the local military commander, mayor and anyone else who considered himself a local dignitary. It could be a time consuming exercise.

For the duty officer it was always a time of hanging about the gangway waiting for senior officers to come and go to salute them, in the time-honoured fashion, over the side. It was whilst waiting my Captain's lunch guests I noticed a local boat approaching the ship – the last in the line of three vessels at anchor but the ship nearest the landing stage ashore. In it was an absolutely stunning young lady attired in hot pants* which were all the rage at the time.

I hadn't been briefed to expect any young ladies that lunch time so was not a little interested as she daintily stepped up the short gangway to the ship's quarter-deck where I was killing time as the Officer of the Day. She was a delightful English rose and inquired if she was on HMS TENBY as, if so, she had a lunch appointment with the Captain. Thinking she must be half blind to miss our ship's stern name board – in huge letters - clearly identifying which ship she was onboard just yards away from where we were standing. I was just about to politely explain that, No Madam this is EASTBOURNE but that the TENBY was anchored a few yards further ahead. Before I could utter the first word I noted my Captain at my elbow who instantly confirmed that despite what we all knew, she wasn't mistaken… she was on the TENBY… and he was expecting her for lunch. In my mind I knew that certainly the chef and steward were not!

As he whisked her away towards his cabin he was no doubt over the moon that he had 'pulled the wool' over one of his fellow Commanding Officers in the Squadron. Whilst he settled down with his other guests and his steward hastily prepared an extra lunch his fellow Commanding Officer just a few yards away doubtless spent most of his lunch hour hovering around his ship's gangway area looking for his expected but absent guest.

The lady concerned turned out to be someone who in later life was to be the wife of a UK Defence minister – but that's a different story. She had come to Istanbul to seek out a relative who was in a local Turkish prison and was going to do her best to get him out (I always wondered if she was expecting one of the visiting HM Ships to oblige in some way). She became quite a resident in the wardroom throughout the following days. Even after sailing from Istanbul to the Turkish Naval Officers academy a short hop down the coast – there she was again. We never did get to hear if she achieved her objective.

So… eyes widened by the Istanbul experience it was time to sail back to the UK for refit after a short stops in Malta, Palermo and Gibraltar..... After a number of breakdowns the ship was certainly ready for some attention in Devonport dock-yard so a gentle passage was planned at a moderate speed. As the UK came ever

---

*For those not familiar with the term 'hot pants', they were an agreeable fashion of the era, comprising tiny shorts that had the appearance of being glued to the wearer.

closer other ships of the squadron (TENBY, SCARBOROUGH and TORQUAY) headed for the Bay of Biscay as part of their training programme but also to say a fond farewell to their sister ship who would be out of the training business for some six months.

To emphasise the point that repairs were much needed as EASTBOURNE prepared to sail past the other ships of the squadron all the oars from the ships three whalers (and the spares) were mustered on the quarterdeck and then taken through the "Burma Road" (the main internal passageway that runs the length of any warship). With much" juggling" to get a lengthy oar through various doors and into every available compartment they were then available to be shoved through a scuttle (porthole) at a co-ordinated order. Then, as the ships steamed past each other, a rowing action was attempted with the timing being beaten out by the First Lieutenant on the bridge roof banging a hug gong, that had been found somewhere on board, trying hard to get some co-ordinated rowing underway! (see photograph).

By now I had nearly completed five years service as a Royal Naval officer and, should I had so wished, I could have called it a day and returned to civilian life after what was really a very short period of time indeed. The years had flown past. Should I or shouldn't I leave, was a constant question going round in my head… What had the Navy taught me? Would civilian employers want me? Had I seen enough of the world? Did I want to 'settle down'? Decisions… decisions…decisions. I was going to have to make up my mind shortly.

What future?

Just days after settling on the blocks back in dry dock back in Devonport the phone in the Captain's cabin rang. Without asking, someone ashore had found another job for me. It seemed Seaman officers always had to be at sea – there was to be no time in which to take a deep breath and enjoy the delight of a more normal life ashore – if only for a few weeks.

Berthed for many months, if not years, in Devonport dockyard was a solitary minesweeper of the same class as I had left in Malta – the good ship CARHAMPTON. She had returned from overseas service, doubtless refitted, but then placed in reserve and mothballed – her future unknown.

At that time the powers that be decided that CARHAMPTON was needed at sea again but a crew had to be rustled together from somewhere. Doubtless another manpower crisis existed so a crew had to be made up from here and there – wherever spare manpower could be identified. A major shipping strike had been under-

way for many weeks at this time so a Merchant Navy Royal Naval Reserve officer was easily found to command her and another – Paul Davies - as a spare hand
cum First Lieutenant cum watchkeeper. It was all pretty vague. I was made available as the third watchkeeper needed to get the vessel to sea.

The first requirement for her was to appear at Hastings as the Navy's representative at the 900th celebrations of the 1066 'event' well remembered in that town.
Hastings can never be described as a port but with a pier – complete with funfair,
bingo hall and Wimpy Bar - it was agreed could accommodate a Ton class
minesweeper – just!

Pottering up channel from Devonport to fly the White Ensign at the celebrations
was no quiet overnight trip. Huge lumps of cocooning (special protective coat-
ings on wooden frames placed over weapons and many other items of upper deck
equipment to prevent corrosion attacking whilst a ship was laid up) were
wrenched off the equipment being protected and simply dumped overboard in
sizeable quantities. Bad news if a yachtsman was following somewhere astern…

Having been laid up for a considerable period of time the ship wasn't exactly
looking its best, as would normally be the case for such a high profile ship visit.
In more normal circumstances tins of grey paint would have appeared and everything in sight be given a quick coat to make sure everything looked 'shipshape
and Bristol fashion'. With no paint onboard washing up liquid was the next best
option. Buckets were produced and every piece of the upper deck structure given
a good wash down. Not ideal, but the best that could be done in the circumstances. The ship arrived at the Hastings pier looking what at best could be called
'average' – certainly no better.

During the first lunchtime secured to the pier the wardroom filled with all those
performers, led by Lance Percival, 'starring' in the summer show close by (amazing how quickly word spread in the dressing rooms, that an HM ship was nearby
– complete with a duty free bar).

As hospitality was doled out in appropriate tumblers and glasses a worried looking senior engineer appeared to seek out the Captain. He was concerned that
every twenty seconds a large thump was felt throughout the ship. If you ever look
at a chart of the area you will see that the available water at the end of the pier
can at best be described as 'minimal', even at high tide. Further investigation con-
cluded that there was so little water under the keel that the smallest of waves was
lifting the whole ship to be afloat one minute and then returning her to be fully
grounded with a good thump the next. Not recommended in the maker's instructions! To answer the worried engineer's queries he was told to put the ship's

screws in the docking position (to prevent damage)… and the party could continue!

The 'seabed encounter' was experienced twice a day for the rest of the visit with minimal interest from anyone else onboard thereafter. The damage would only be spotted at the ship's next docking and, who by then, would remember the visit to Hastings?

After a few weeks I was back onboard EASTBOURNE after my loan to CARHAMPTON. My feet were not to stay still for long…

With a name like EASTBOURNE and 'adopted' by the same town it wasn't too difficult to appreciate why the ship was asked to provide a judge for the Miss Southern Television competition being held in the town that summer. I guess as the only bachelor amongst the wardroom team (I was the youngest by several years) I was the natural choice to head to Eastbourne a few weeks later to be a judge in what was obviously a needle beauty contest on the south coast circuit – and televised too.

Again, although not Dartmouth trained for such a role, I appeared, resplendent in my uniform, to do my best seated on the stage with a row of B list celebrities (from local TV and Equity yellow pages no doubt). I was very open with these good judges that really I had little idea how to mark the beauties that were about to be seen by us all – in swimsuits and then in long evening dresses. Sat alongside me was a 'celebrity' whose name is best omitted here. He was obviously a pro at these sort of affairs and advised me that on a first viewing of the girls I should just spot one who took my fancy and then just juggle all the various headings for appropriate markings on my score sheet (charm, deportment, appearance etc) to make my girl win. This I did… I spotted what I thought was a very appropriate young lady and then awarded her some highly inflated scores to make her stand head and shoulders above the rest. I had undoubtedly picked a winner I told myself.

Around twenty lovely ladies appeared on the stage and did their bit. Within minutes of the final parade the score sheets were collected and someone back stage did the arithmetic. I looked relaxed and looked forward to my girl being announced as the winner!

I am ashamed to report that with only five other judges reporting, my lass came in a miserable eleventh. I obviously have a lot to learn in this area but having picked one of the shortest girls on stage to be my winner I later established I had made a major mistake… apparently tall is best in this game! I have never been asked to judge such a similar event since so I can only put my newfound knowledge to good use to you dear reader. You never know - one day perhaps?

CHAPTER NINETEEN

STEADY AS SHE GOES CAP'N

You have guessed it – as the summer ticked by and I made every effort to visit my stunning new nurse girlfriend from Paignton my own senior officers seemed to be making every effort to get me back to sea in the opposite direction! They eventually won! I suppose I should have expected it; I was a seaman officer with not a lot to do, with the ship in dry dock being crawled over by engineers.

This time the call from the local Flag Officer's office indicated a ship – LOFOTEN – in Falmouth had to land an officer as a result of a serious medical condition. I was to be despatched to make up the numbers. My first job was to look up in an appropriate reference book what this ship LOFOTEN was all about. I had never heard of her.

She did warrant a reference in my books and a photo showed she was a World War II vintage Landing Ship (Tank) in naval terminology. But, the small print revealed that after many years in reserve along with many sister ships she, unlike most of the others, got the call for further sea service as the remainder headed for the scrapyard.

At that time the Navy was introducing a new submarine-hunting helicopter into service – the Wessex Mk 3. It was going to be the answer to many problems at sea as the Soviets built up their submarine force at an alarming rate at the height of the Cold War. Actually these helicopters also had a major problem themselves. In order for their sonar – dipped into the sea whilst sub hunting – to be at its most effective really deep water was needed. The local waters round the UK coast, which are relatively shallow in submarine terms, were simply not acceptable.

The urgent requirement was to get the helicopter crews to train in deep waters but to do so they couldn't just fly out from the naval air station at Culdrose on the Lizard peninsula in Cornwall, exercise for an hour and then fly home. It was too far and they didn't have the fuel capacity to remain on task for more than a few minutes so far from home. The answer was to provide them with fuel one hundred or more miles off Land's End where the depth of water increases dramatically. There was thus a requirement for a new 'aircraft carrier' to be built or at least converted from existing tonnage then available. The latter option was chosen and LOFOTEN was hauled into dock from the reserve fleet to be converted for a new role. Whilst her crew frequently called her 'Britain's latest aircraft carrier' she was in reality little more than a floating petrol station able to get herself slowly – 7 knots was a good speed for her - into position in deep water to dispense aviation fuel as required for her visiting helicopters.

Briefed as to her role, I had, as usual, just twenty-four hours to recover my clothes from the laundry, pack a bag and head for Falmouth arriving in a navy staff car from Plymouth on a very quiet Sunday morning.

The ship lay peacefully at the Queen's Wharf with the only movement seen onboard being a few seagulls lurking hopefully near the food waste chutes rigged over the stern. Gingerly stepping on a huge gangway and easing my bags and body onboard I was met by not a soul. The Quartermaster responsible for the security of the ship had wandered off so I was free to wander off to get my bearings, leaving my bags in the gangway area. They could be collected later.

Internally the huge ship revealed itself and I soon found the wardroom where my guess was that the duty officer would be found scanning the Sunday papers or, perchance, enjoying a pre-lunch snooze? Glancing inside – there was no officer to be seen but a senior rating sat at the bar idly eating peanuts on his own. I should say at this point that at this time in the Royal Navy no alcohol was permitted onboard except for commissioned officers who alone had the privilege of drinking the stuff. Sailors, and that included senior ratings, had to satisfy themselves with their daily tot of rum. Here I was, being greeted by a senior rating inviting me into what was to be my home – and offering me a Gin and Tonic too! Just a little odd I reasoned. Anxious to know what was going on I gently asked for the whereabouts of the duty officer. Somewhat sheepishly mine host – who I actually recognised from earlier days at sea in the minesweepers in Malta – said that 'there is a bit of a party on at Culdrose this lunchtime so I'm looking out for him.'

What? Often any sizeable ship will reduce down to just one officer onboard when sat alongside in port but even on Christmas day there is one duty officer nominated and onboard – never drinking with his chums twenty miles away.

It was an interesting introduction to life onboard. To kill the time till the party-goers returned for a late lunch I found a nominal list of officers who were to be my fellow messmates for the next couple of months. A perusal of the list and some research over the coming days indicated this ship was not officered by many, if any, who were destined for high rank one-day. Officers onboard had, it seemed, been appointed to this very ancient vessel rather than being shown the big door to a civilian life ashore. All seemed to have a skeleton in the cupboard of some sort.

The Captain I noted had served something like a massive seventeen years as a Lieutenant Commander. Surely some record. All his contemporaries who joined up with him had either made it to a much higher rank – or were farming in Suffolk. He obviously had salt in his veins and was happy to remain in the service and at sea. Such people did and still do exist – they all tend to be 'characters'. The Navy needs them too!

Leaving the Royal Yacht after an unidentified incident qualified one officer for an instant job onboard LOFOTEN; another had recently left an Australian aircraft carrier where he had been the second officer of the watch when she had literally chopped a destroyer in half during a major exercise. There was obviously a great loss of life. Another failed a Hydrographic course; another, an aviator, was told after some career interview or other he must hardly be seen standing next to a Fleet Air Arm aircraft – certainly never fly one! and so the list went on. Sounds an interesting team, I mused, as I settled into my new home... I thought hard what I may have done wrong in the past few weeks to be onboard. Perhaps it was no more than not being fully employed on a ship in refit?

On Monday we slipped our berthing wires, ventured out into the beautiful Falmouth harbour and headed for my first, and the ship's final, appointment with a couple of helicopters. They used the deck for some landing practice, doubtless for trainee pilots, for an hour, whilst we onboard encouraged the engineers to give us their best as far as speed was concerned. We were heading for Portland – not a million miles away but here, in the speed department, LOFOTEN had a problem. Those who knew about these things as being a 'Steam Reciprocating' system described her machinery. As any engineer will tell you it was a very basic wartime emergency arrangement whereby steam was produced from a conventional boiler and then used to propel an amazing system of pistons, beams and con rods that in turn eventually drove the two propeller shafts. Whilst interesting to watch, as a piece of very ancient maritime history, steam oozed from brackets and glands… speed through the water was never the end result. I think the fastest ever recorded during my time onboard was a mere eight knots (10 mph) and that was on a good day - with the wind astern! If the wind and tide were unkind the same effort from down below in Dante's inferno frequently saw the ship make absolutely zero progress over the ground for hour after hour until the wind or tide – or both – slackened.

With Portland Bill spotted ahead, eventually (I think the same day!) it was abeam and we rounded the well-known mariners landmark for the run into Portland Harbour, the engines huffing and puffing steam everywhere. Para Handy eat your heart out!

Our next appointment at Portland was simple. The ship was, at least nominally, a member of the Second Frigate Squadron based at the Dorset port. Somehow or other someone had persuaded the Admiral ashore that our old pile of steel would accompany all the latest frigates in the Squadron on an important summer visit to the Baltic. Always the best month to visit and the girls were always known for their welcome! We were all up for it, but before sailing – at least a day before the others - we had one more role to fulfil.

Every summer the Portland Squadron, as they were also known, threw a mega cocktail party for the good and great of south Dorset – and their own wives and girlfriends. The venue was always the problem as individual ships were too small to cope with the numbers involved.

Solution… invite LOFOTEN along and use her extensive flat flight deck over the tank deck for the party… and find a friendly Army officer somewhere to locate a suitable marquee to cover the whole deck.

After much phoning about the place some weeks earlier a suitable source of tentage was identified and, on arrival at Q Pier Portland, a small squad of lads from the Army base at Bovingdon were awaiting to erect their massive tent. This was no job for a bunch of boy scouts; it was huge and obviously normally all the guy ropes and other paraphernalia were secured to the ground using steel pegs. Onboard a ship however things were somewhat different and alternative arrangements had to be made to secure the whole thing down. No fixture, fitting or guardrail escaped – everything was pressed into service as an anchoring point for this huge marquee. Even the ship's funnel was considered at one point. The big question was, what would happen if the wind got up strength as it so frequently does at Portland. Many fingers (and toes) remained firmly crossed.

On the day of the race the weather was perfect. The tent was bedecked with flowers, piles of food and drinks imported and the ship was ready to throw a party…. a big party.

As a new boy who had only been onboard a week or so I was obviously the prime candidate to be on duty so that all the regulars onboard could entertain their guests. I was none too fussed, as it was a beautiful evening, absolutely ideal for the event.

For the first hour at least it was simply a time to stand at the top of the gangway with a fixed smile and almost permanent salute. 'Good evening… welcome onboard… nice to see you… welcome… good evening,' and so it went on as everyone stepped onboard. Whilst semi brain dead for the welcoming routine it was an excellent time to do some basic people watching, with thoughts such as, ' He should invest in a dinner jacket three sizes bigger,' or 'Why is she wearing shoes like that to come onboard a ship?' or 'Is that his wife or his daughter?' or repetitive thoughts about mutton being dressed as lamb… It kept the brain active whilst going through the motions of welcoming guests onboard, none of whom, as the new boy, I recognised.

Once the partygoers were safely onboard it was time to escape the gangway and try to locate a salad or something similar that the chef had left out for us duty-men.

Escaping to an empty wardroom I caught up on the TV news and then started clock watching for the guests to start to leave. They were literally having a ball… everyone else onboard just had a long night ahead. Our turn would come, we told ourselves – we were heading for the Baltic soon when someone else could do the duty!

Eventually those with baby-sitters to relieve started to make their exit so it was time to head for the gangway again and repeat the welcoming routine with only the words altered to wish everyone a pleasant trip home and thank them for coming. Only as the last stragglers drifted off much later than expected did the words come for the last half dozen of them through gritted teeth.

With the clock being nearer to 0200 than midnight it was then just a job to round up our own officers and see them all safely heading for their beds before the duty day could end. It was a beautiful night and fortified by an evening's entertainment there was, unfortunately, no need for any of them to instantly head off to bed. They were on home ground – the party could continue. Most of the wardroom members drifted down to the stern of the vessel and relaxed and chatted as they complimented themselves on a party well hosted.

My sober mutterings and suggestions about an 'early' night fell on deaf ears. Oh, for some rain to clear them off below decks but there was no chance of that. It was just a beautiful June night.

At some stage the Captain piped up and, for no reason as far as I could make out, started to verbally hassle our excellent young Midshipman onboard at that time. He got both barrels, poor lad. 'You know your trouble,' barked the Captain, 'you have no guts, determination or drive. You'll never make a half decent naval officer.' Phew! The Midshipman, quite understandably, remained silent. It was of course the beer talking.

The Captain started his second salvo off by hurling, 'When I was a Mid, if any Captain of mine had told me I had no guts, determination or drive I would have thrown the old coot into the sea.'

Nothing else was said. The Midshipman, a good fly half in the ship's rugby team, simply stepped the three necessary paces forward, picked up the Captain round his waist, well clear of the deck, and with one heave he was heading twenty feet or more down into the murky waters of Portland Harbour – and all in his best uniform too...

Panic stations! Whilst the other partygoers stood around either congratulating the Midshipman or simply querying if that was the best way to end the party I rushed away to find the other (hopefully) sober member of the ship's company that night – the quartermaster guarding the gangway. Shouting for him to find a heaving line we both rushed for an area of the ship's side that had metal bars welded to it forming wide steps down to the waterline. They were rungs left over from the ship's earlier life as a Landing Ship, which commandos would have used to board their smaller landing craft alongside. Three cheers that no one had decided to remove them during the ship's 'aircraft carrier' refit.

Heading down the rusty rungs in our best uniforms we were soon close to sea level and could see the Captain spluttering away to our right. He too could see his escape route and was coming our way, thankfully! Nothing like an early morning salt-water bath to revive flagging spirits or bring back memories of earlier swimming lessons! He eventually grabbed our lifeline and was hauled to the ship's side ready to be lifted aloft.

His swim had focussed the attention of the others to the time and by the time our illustrious captain had returned to the upper deck it was clear of partygoers. A wet trail towards his cabin was the only evidence remaining so it was at last time to follow him - to my bunk for a much later than anticipated appointment.

Next day someone else was on duty as a major clear up got underway and by the end of the day with the tent down LOFOTEN looked more like a warship again.

Mid morning the Captain, who kept a motorbike onboard, was ashore heading back to his home in Plymouth and the ship and her crew could relax for what remained of the weekend.

By mid afternoon however the Captain's wife was on the phone asking where her husband was.... I knew he had left four or five hours earlier and in plenty of time to get back to Plymouth on his fine bike. We feared the worse but there was little we could do. He had escaped drowning earlier that day – had he now been involved in some ghastly road accident? It was a possibility on everyone's mind.

It was close to 2300 when the phone rang again for the duty officer. It was the Captain's wife again... all was well, he had just got home – she had obviously been a worried lady. The story was that, as he was a little tired, (we understood that bit) he had stopped his bike somewhere in Dorset, climbed over a farmer's gate for an hour's shut eye and woke some five or six hours later, fully refreshed, but somewhat behind schedule as he headed on to Plymouth.

By Monday all was forgotten and the ship steamed out of Portland Harbour heading for Sweden. Nothing, as far as I know, was said regarding the Midshipman's lack of initiative or the subsequent swimming episode in Portland harbour. It was time to head for Malmo and join up with all the smart vessels of the Second Frigate Squadron for a long-awaited official visit.

As is often the case, shortly after arriving in port, it was time for some members of the ships company to be whisked away to view the local brewery and sample some of the products at the end of their tour whilst the ships officers prepared themselves for a busy evening ahead. For them the next duty was to host the official cocktail party thrown by the local Royal Naval attaché - in town for the weekend from Stockholm. As ships officers we were on hand to act as hosts whilst he entertained his military and business contacts that had been invited onboard for the occasion.To ships officers one cocktail party is very much like the next but they can be difficult if there is a language problem or the entire guest list is taken from the town hall phone book. For local residents they are a much appreciated opportunity to step onboard one of her Majesty's ships. Young officers always make a dive for the last page of the guest list when it arrives onboard from the Embassy to see if any young ladies had been added to the list. (They did us proud in Malmo – enough said?)

Duty once again – they came round frequently - I was once again the officer greeting the guests at the top of the gangway with a fixed smile and same old words of welcome. "Good evening… Thank you for coming… Good evening… Nice to see you… Good evening….." alongside my Captain.

Half way through the ritual arrival and in the midst of all the smiles and salutes the duty Petty Officer arrived in the vicinity of the gangway at great speed and looking more than a little concerned. As my arm went up and down saluting he was right alongside me saying. "Quick Sir… come down to the tank deck (the junior rates accommodation area in the rebuilt ship) we've had a murder". His message was clear and it was time to escape the gangway and race below to the tank deck……. Sure enough laying spread across the deck was a sailor face down in a huge pool of blood - the pool getting rapidly bigger all the time. Through his neck was a standard navy rigging knife complete with its blade of some six inches in length.

Whilst others attended the man on the deck I raced back to the cocktail party to find a doctor if at all possible. It was a difficult exercise. Appearing at someone's elbow I would gabble after my rush back to the upper deck " Excuse me… are you a doctor" only for my query to be returned by almost a formal handshake and something like "I am Mr Carl Andersson, it is good to meet you… I am the local Police Inspector.. and this is my wife…." I had already moved on… and so it went on and on. Eventually medical assistance was found … an ambulance called and I returned to the gangway convinced I had done my best at the scene of an attempted murder. (History records that the knifing had taken place after some of those returning from the brewery had decided to return ashore again but one, already a duty watch member had asked his chum returning from the brewery if he would continue to substitute for him on the duty roster. He declined. The next demand was simple…. "Do my watch or I'll stick this **** knife through your neck". The reply "Yer Ok then big man" or some such similar comment saw the knife grabbed and thrust though the man's neck as promised. It was all over in a flash.)

Whilst a man fought for his life on the tank deck, the Gin and Tonic fuelled small talk continued at the cocktail party - few noticing the eventual transfer of the man ashore on a stretcher and him being rushed to the local hospital for emergency treatment. (History again records that the man concerned was returned to UK under escort and eventually sentenced to some six months in Naval Detention Quarters for his hasty and stupid action that balmy June evening in Sweden)

Leaving harbour on completion of the visit the frigates were soon just a speck on the horizon as they raced away for their next round of training exercises whilst we resorted to watching the Danish coastline slowly, very slowly, pass by as we headed for another few days of wonderful Norwegian hospitality in Kristiansand. Can you beat southern Norway in June to see that part of Scandinavia at it's best? At least at these speeds all our paperwork was always up to date and In Trays empty when we arrived in our next port of call.

Norway - the ships last foreign visit was soon over and it was back to chug… hiss… chug… hiss… Hour after hour, day after day it went on as the ancient machinery installed during the dark days of World War II – doubtless for an expected single journey only – was still wheezing away over twenty years later.

Going on watch with Dover harbour just a mile or two to starboard encouraged everyone that we were nearing home at last. The only problem was Dover was still there some four hours later at the end of the watch too. The tide was obviously heading in the wrong direction for us!

Surely, with a following breeze beginning to rise, we would soon say goodbye to the cross channel ferries slipping past. They probably thought we had anchored outside the port. A wind from astern may have helped a little but with the open bridge of this class of ship at the same height as the top of the funnel just a few feet astern the wind was in exactly the wrong direction for us on the bridge. The bridge was soon full of the main boiler exhaust gases – neat sulphur as far as I was concerned – and definitely not a pleasant or healthy experience. A change of course in such circumstances was necessary as, like a sailing ship, we tacked down channel to keep the horrific fumes outboard. I'm sure other shipping in the channel that day were more than interested in why we were acting like a sail training vessel rather than an aircraft carrier changing course every half hour or so.

A couple of days later, after another brief visit to Portland, we edged into Plymouth Sound and up into the naval base. I dare not commit to paper all the antics that took place that final night at sea. Those involved will remember and it is probably best left like that!

As the main engines were rung off for the last time (30th June 1967) LOFOTEN had, at long last, ended her seagoing career. Within a few days everyone had left and she was soon abandoned, an empty hulk, at buoys in the harbour awaiting her eventual fate in a breakers yard. But the memories remain, even decades later. Good old LOFOTEN and her amazing crew!

It was again time to find my proper ship still lurking in the dockyard somewhere – what an interlude my fellow messmates had missed!

CHAPTER TWENTY

TORREY CANYON

Although in theory still a junior officer in a frigate in refit at Devonport I was rapidly considering myself as some sort of nautical gypsy when yet another temporary appointment loomed – and always it seemed to be an overnight requirement that had to be filled.

The now infamous tanker TORREY CANYON (of some 118,000 tons), whilst en route from the Middle East to the oil terminals of Milford Haven juddered to a halt when she hit the Seven Stones reef off Land's End. Within minutes her cargo of thick black oil started to escape into the seas around her. Within hours the currents were taking the black gold in every direction. Every Cornish beach was threatened.

Within a few days I was also en route to Falmouth – again – to join a small Inshore minesweeper ODIHAM. She had been despatched to the port with basically a civilian crew – including women (very rare if not unheard of in those days) - from the now defunct Royal Naval Auxiliary Service. Looking down from the Western Wharf in Falmouth docks as I arrived for yet another 'fill in' job, I eventually found her berthed many feet below me. I was getting used to it and I was to be the only RN person onboard this one.

There were already many of these small vessels at Falmouth ready to be despatched to spray the TORREY CANYON oil which was working its way round the coast from the Seven Stones reef in massive quantities.

Trainloads of detergent arrived in Falmouth docks overnight, every night. There had never been a maritime accident like this anywhere around the UK coast so no dormant organisation or preplanning existed. It was simply a case of running the whole operation as events presented themelves on a daily basis. In hindsight, a helicopter could easily have gone up daily from the nearby Culdrose Naval airbase to spot the oil and direct us in the minesweepers to it. We would then have been able to spray it furiously.

What actually happened was we were fitted with temporary booms to spray our detergent on any oil spotted and we were sailed early every day looking for it. Our height of eye onboard was so low it meant on some days we never even saw a drop of the thick black stuff. The orders were however that we were not allowed back into harbour until we had used all our detergent – so, on a blank day when no oil was spotted, I hate to report that, pretty exhausted after a long day bouncing around in the channel looking for the stuff, we simply threw our forty-gallon drums of detergent over the side so we could go back to harbour for a meal and rest… before doing it all again the next day!

When we did find and spray oil – always by accident rather than advanced planning - we furiously pumped detergent into it, in the hope it would break down the oil and it would all simply sink. Time and the tides would eventually break it all up. That was the theory at least!

Going to the heads (toilets) onboard was somewhat out of the normal. We would flush the system in the normal way but by return we would receive neat black TORREY CANYON oil into the pan! Nice, eh? The detergent was viscous stuff and for many years to follow I had an eye problem from working with so much of the wretched stuff in the atmosphere. Either the oil or detergent did a good job paint stripping on our ship's sides too, in some places removing the accumulation of many years of paint right back to the original wooden hull.

The job went on for a few weeks – as the Fleet Air Arm bombed the tanker in the hope that the remaining fuel could be set alight and thus dispersed. It never really seemed to work but the pilots doubtless enjoyed their Easter holidays lobbing 1,000lb bombs at the ship's hull rapidly turning it into a pile of scrap above, though mainly below, the surface. It was reported that of the forty-two bombs aimed at the tanker thirty hit home – an excellent couple of days work. The remaining fuel never did catch light despite the efforts of the Fleet Air Arm's best

– with some help from napalm delivered by the Royal Air Force Hunters flying from North Devon.

All these things eventually come to an end, as did the oil spraying. It was no great loss to be back on board EASTBOURNE again but I always blame that whole interlude for coming between a very attractive nurse from Paignton and me - working at Plymouth's Freedom Fields hospital. Lucy Dinham was definitely a girl to set the heart racing at the time but naval life didn't help and, after a short stay working in a London hospital, she eventually flew to Vancouver Canada and doubtless met some other shore-based guy – sensible girl! My loss, his gain no doubt. I wish them both well but if that officer on the bridge of the TORREY CANYON had been a better navigator than he was... who knows how things would have developed............ 'All part of life in a blue suit,' I was frequently told by my so-called sympathetic messmates.

CHAPTER TWENTY-ONE

OUT OF REFIT ... AT LAST!

During my summer of unexpected 'fill in' jobs whilst all the married officers onboard enjoyed their break in and around the Devon countryside, Devonport Dockyard, eventually, completed the refit of Her Majesty's warship EASTBOURNE. She was ready to renew her role as a young officers' training ship for the Britannia RN College at Dartmouth. Spic and span inside and out again.

Before the ship took up its training role, trials and exercises had to be undertaken to satisfy all concerned that the Dockyard had indeed done a good job and all the work expected had been done to the highest standards.

It was a Friday night... most of the dockyard workers had headed home but with the ship's programme running a few weeks late it was essential that every opportunity be taken to complete every trial whatever day of the week it was.

The first and pretty basic trial was one to prove that after many months out of use and with various work having been undertaken to all the machinery it all actually worked and was capable of driving the ship through the seas in the weeks and months ahead.

Leaving Devonport at the end of the working day the plan was to make a simple overnight passage across the channel round Jersey and back into Devonport the following morning. Nothing too stressful but a good initial run for the engineers to check everything below worked as planned.

On leaving harbour speed was initially ordered for just ten knots and as the engineers reported that all was well speed was to be increased – with revolutions for a further five knots ordered at any appropriate time.

It was flat calm and a wonderful night, and it felt good be back at sea with all the dockyard cobwebs being blown away after many months in a dry dock.

Rostered for the First watch (from 2000 – 2359) I was looking forward to the first early supper since refit from a new and enthusiastic team of chefs and stewards. I could feel through the decks slight vibration that speed was being gradually increased as I enjoyed my meal with all the normal banter of mess life going on around me.

No time for a coffee… it was time to leap below to get my normal watchkeeping kit – torch, weatherproof jacket and a Mars bar for later on as midnight approached. It would doubtless be a quiet night for the bridge staff whilst the engineers carefully watched all their equipment and machinery.

Soon on the bridge my predecessor was happy to brief me on the shipping situation round about me through the bridge windows. He could doubtless pick up the smells of dinner wafting up the ladder so was keen not to linger. A quick look at the radar and he showed me a much larger than usual contact ten, maybe twenty miles, further down channel to the west of us. I made the assumption with a contact showing that big on the radar it must be a super tanker – at least. I easily decided it would be no problem where it was and what we were proposing to do. A mental note was made of the other contacts showing and a visual update was soon explained to me. Navigation was no problem – we were heading for a point almost mid Channel. Speed had gradually been increased during my predecessors watch and we were by now zipping along at a healthy twenty knots, a speed at which the miles would soon pass on that night's proposed cross-Channel dash.

I was told to expect a call from the engine room when they were happy to go up the final increase of power to some twenty-five knots – a speed approaching full power.

The call soon came and I gave the orders for the increase in power. The Captain who had been about the bridge keeping an eye on things on this, his first day back at sea with the wind in his face, waited until the ship's log showed the increase of speed had been achieved when he too decided it was time to go below for his supper.

All was calm on the bridge – the ship was doing exactly what the engineers wanted and at this speed there was unlikely to be any shipping that could have been considered a danger. Lights from fishing boats, pleasure craft heading for a weekend in France or the Channel Islands were all clearly to be seen around me – I thought!

And then it all happened… with no notice the whole ship started violently to shake as if held in the hand of a mighty sea monster. A glance astern saw masses of black smoke billowing from the funnel and blown clear by the ship's forward movement, which soon started to gradually reduce. We had lost all power to our screws and were slowing down minute by minute. With telephones ringing, intercoms crackling and then all electrical power failing - things were happening fast. I flew through the starboard bridge wing door to hoist the Not Under Command lights outside and to the rear of the bridge. These two vertical red lights are always held ready for emergency use to warn any vessel in the area to keep clear. In my dash to the signal deck and the appropriate lights I just saw it out of the corner of my eye… A very large vessel with navigation lights far higher than I would normally expect… where had she come from? Was this the 'super tanker' I had spotted on radar as I came on watch? If so she had some turn of speed! In a matter of seconds all in one's watchkeeping experience changed dramatically...

My instinct told me I had to turn towards the fast approaching set of lights and attempt to go round the vessel's stern. By now our speed was doubtless down to some fifteen knots… the funnel was still shaking and the black smoke although still in evidence was reducing. 99% of those on duty that night were doubtless concerned at what defect we had in the engine and boiler room. Others could worry about that… I was much more interested in the ship that was obviously very close to me – far closer than I dared admit. The sweat was on both my forehead and spine. What should I do next…? I knew I should call my captain but by the time he arrived it could well have been too late. I had to act…..

With very little electrical power available but with the wheel over to starboard the ship was gently turning that way… slowly. I glanced at the radar to see how close this ship was. It was so close it didn't even show on the screen! There was very little I could do except let our ship keep swinging to starboard; according to international collision regulations the best direction in which to head. In seconds I appreciated that I was going to, just, miss hitting this huge vessel, as it was travelling at great speed and aft of her all important navigation lights she was lit up like a Christmas tree. We were very close but turning away. It had been a very close thing. As I began to appreciate that my 'super tanker' was in fact some large cruise liner the signalman on watch with me grabbed a signal lantern powered by an emergency power supply and aimed it at the ship passing rapidly before our eyes. Through the dark night we could both pick out the letters above us.

Q..U..E..E..N.. the light showed us… M..A..R..Y..

On occasions like this you do have to stop and literally thank God for preservation from a very near major catastrophe at sea. Two hundred or more men could easily have gone to the sea bed that night as the mighty transatlantic liner, making her routine dash from New York to Southampton, sliced a little frigate in half. (She had unfortunately done so in World War II when in service as a fast troop transport sinking HMS CURACAO.) I often wonder if her officers took much notice of a radar contact that one minute was showing navigation lights, the next none, and all within a mile or so of them as the mighty liner pounded up channel. Nothing gets in the way of any ship at speed, was doubtless their thought pattern, as it had been mine just half an hour earlier.

Back on my own ship obvious great concern and interest was being shown in our breakdown, the restoration of essential electrical power and if we should continue round Jersey as planned. Only the signalman and I knew what happened on the bridge that night – and I have never mentioned the incident myself!

It was over in minutes… and the liner was soon out of sight. Doubtless the band played on.

Before turning in for the night the Captain reappeared. 'All well up here?' he enquired, now that the engineers, who had been his first priority for a couple of hours, were all happy again below decks. The lights were on and speed was slowly being increased again.

'Yes sir, fine. All quiet up here,' as we continued our simple overnight cruise round Jersey……

Having recovered from the QUEEN MARY incident and shaken off the dockyard cobwebs - and workers - it was soon time to start training young officers and ratings again. For the Autumn cruise the programme was not planned to take the ship far from the UK coastline.....

Come November however we were bashing against wind and weather up the English channel in a Force 10 gale heading for the safe haven of Portsmouth naval base. As light was beginning to fail for the day a distress call was received onboard that red flares had been seen just one mile south of Brook Point on the Isle of Wight. Being just 8 miles to the south we steamed off at our best safe speed to investigate.....

In very poor light and weather conditions we eventually found the Swedish registered MV LENNART broken down but under partial sail just a mile off the coast on a lee shore (She was thus in eminent danger of being blown ashore and wrecked)

An RAF Rescue helicopter from nearby Thorney Island was on the scene and attempting to rescue the crew. The priority was the owners young wife – a Mrs Sarah Vought - who was over 8 months pregnant. Normally the helicopter would lower a crewman to the vessel...attach a rescue strop to the casualty and then both would be lifted clear of the ship and to safety. At only 100 tons and with two masts gyrating wildly in a full gale it was an impossible task to use their normal procedures. The only hope was for Mrs Vought to jump into the boiling November seas to hopefully drift clear of her ship and then to be snatched from the sea by the helicopter crew. Bravely she did as her rescuers demanded but not before disappearing into the accommodation area of the vessel to grab a heavy winters coat which she put on before jumping......she thought it was her only hope and that of her soon to be delivered baby.

Within a very few minutes she had indeed been snatched from the sea and myself and two others were on the bows of our ship pitching into the wild seas. Roped on for our own safety the ship was dipping into the seas at the entire height of her forward upper deck so at times we were at sea level –and then way above it. People paid money for this at the fun fair back ashore – but never in such dangerous conditions as this. With great skill the helicopter pilot lowered her into our grasp – but she was barely conscious.A large semi conscious lady on a gyrating deck was not an easy exercise to bring to a successful conclusion....and we had no midwife either! It had been a narrow escape. Whilst those on the bridge concentrated on taking her ship in tow so close to the shore my small team had to get the good lady along the pitching deck – whilst drifting in and out of consciousness (more out than in) and then up and down steep ladders to the Captain's cabin – the only place onboard with a domestic bath. We simply had to get her body temperature up as quickly as we could. Amazed that her overcoat hadn't drowned her we soon had it off and attempted to get her and her very large bump into a warm bath. She and her bump were getting better but our problem in the prevailing seas was to keep any water in the bath for her. With every pitch and roll most of the water slopped out. If it hadn't been so serious the whole situation was fast in danger of becoming a total comedy!

With her eventually revived, after a long wait, we heard her story that she and her husband had sailed from Gothenburg with a couple of friends – illegally and against all advice - with minimal equipment for a new "good life" in the West Indies. Having been detained in Newhaven for repairs demanded by the UK authorities they had, days earlier to our involvement, sailed from the Sussex port but after over 24 hours adrift and with no idea of their position nearly ended their days on the rocks off the Isle of Wight. With the tow underway and the casualty recovering onboard, within a few hours the vessel was eventually passed to a tug from Portsmouth naval base in the calmer conditions of the Solent. Life soon returned to normal onboard EASTBOURNE. Our trainees and the crew of the LENNART had learnt a lot that day....

History records that some three months later EASTBOURNE was heading for the harbour entrance at Gibraltar on another cruise at exactly the same time as a scruffy looking Swedish motor vessel – it was none other than the good ship LENNART again! Repairs completed and a new baby born to the Vought family they were still determined to make it to the West Indies and a short stay in Gibraltar was all part of their new plan.

Friendships renewed.... it was time for the new baby to be Christened and an invitation to some of the ships company to attend were much appreciated and accepted whilst both vessels stayed briefly in Gibraltar.

What happened to the LENNART and her crew thereafter is unknown but a press report some months later indicated she was again in trouble and her four crew members were again rescued - this time by by a Dutch merchant ship heading for Barbados as the LENNART again wallowed in heavy sea south east of San Juan broken down.

My five years in uniform were just about up.....I had to decide that week...was I to stay in the Navy or seek a civilian career. There was too much excitement around - I decided I would stay for another five years at least...but that could be another story one day!